NEW TESTAMENT MESSAGE

A Biblical-Theological Commentary

Wilfrid Harrington, O.P. and Donald Senior, C.P.

EDITORS

New Testament Message, Volume 21

THE JOHANNINE EPISTLES

Pheme Perkins

Michael Glazier, Inc.
Wilmington, Delaware

MICHAEL GLAZIER, INC.
1210A King Street
Wilmington, Delaware 19801

Library of Congress Catalog Card Number: 79-55808
International Standard Book Number
   New Testament Message Series: 0-89453-123-9
   JOHANNINE EPISTLES: 0-89453-144-1

Printed in the United States of America by Abbey Press

Contents

EDITORS' PREFACE

New Testament Message is a commentary series designed to bring the best of biblical scholarship to a wide audience. Anyone who is sensitive to the mood of the church today is aware of a deep craving for the Word of God. This interest in reading and praying the scriptures is not confined to a religious elite. The desire to strengthen one's faith and to mature in prayer has brought Christians of all types and all ages to discover the beauty of the biblical message. Our age has also been heir to an avalanche of biblical scholarship. Recent archaeological finds, new manuscript evidence, and the increasing volume of specialized studies on the Bible have made possible a much more profound penetration of the biblical message. But the flood of information and its technical nature keeps much of this scholarship out of the hands of the Christian who is eager to learn but is not a specialist. *New Testament Message* is a response to this need.

The subtitle of the series is significant: "A Biblical-Theological Commentary." Each volume in the series, while drawing on up-to-date scholarship, concentrates on bringing to the fore in understandable terms the specific message of each biblical author. The essay-format (rather than a word-by-word commentary) helps the reader savor the beauty and power of the biblical message and, at the same time, understand the sensitive task of responsible biblical interpretation.

A distinctive feature of the series is the amount of space given to the "neglected" New Testament writings, such as Colossians, James, Jude, the Pastoral Letters, the Letters of Peter and John. These briefer biblical books make a significant but often overlooked contribution to the richness of the New Testament. By assigning larger than normal coverage to these books, the series hopes to give these parts of Scripture the attention they deserve.

Because *New Testament Message* is aimed at the entire English speaking world, it is a collaborative effort of international proportions. The twenty-two contributors represent biblical scholarship in North America, Ireland, Britain and Australia. Each of the contributors is a recognized expert in his or her field, has published widely, and has been chosen because of a proven ability to communicate at a popular level. And, while all of the contributors are Roman Catholic, their work is addressed to the Christian community as a whole. The New Testament is the patrimony of all Christians.It is the hope of all concerned with this series that it will bring a fuller appreciation of God's saving Word to his people.

Wilfrid Harrington, O.P.
Donald Senior, C.P.

PREFACE

BECAUSE WE DID NOT WANT to burden the readers of this series with the weight of scholarly debate, many of those to whom I am indebted for my understanding of the Johannine writings will remain anonymous, hidden behind the "some scholars say" and like expressions. The suggested readings at the end will indicate who some of them are, and I trust that the more learned reader will have no difficulty attaching names to the various strands of Johannine scholarship reflected in these pages. I owe a particular debt of gratitude to Donald Senior, one of the editors of the series, who suggested I write this book. Though I have worked on the fourth gospel for some years, it had not occurred to me to try unravelling the perplexities of the Johannine letters. The experience of doing so has proven both more fruitful and more interesting than I might have predicted at the outset. And I trust that the reader will also find more here than his or her initial expectations of such unimposing writings might suggest.

None of the most important insights of the present commentary would have been possible without the fellowship from the *National Endowment for the Humanities* which has been supporting my study of gnostic revelation dialogues. That work is showing how much of the crucial history of christianity in the 2nd and 3rd centuries derives from the complex interaction of literacy and texts with religious communities who understand tradition, authority and even the self, in oral and not literate terms. Our interpretation of the Johannine communities represents part of a much larger refocusing of perspective on 2nd and 3rd cent.

religious movements, which sees the roots of their stories in the context of larger processes of socio-cultural and cognitive change. The third section of the Introduction, "Literary Characteristics of the Letters," contains a rather lengthly discussion of the problems of composition and tradition in such communities. The reader, who simply wishes to get to the interpretation of specific passages, may prefer to skip such theoretical speculations. Perhaps better understanding of this ancient period of religious turmoil will help us sort out our present confusion over evaluating religious claims and cults. The *National Endowment* also made possible a stay in both Egypt and Israel, where it is still possible to observe something of what it would have been like to live in the face-to-face society of the ancient world by observing life in the old quarters of Cairo and Jerusalem and in numerous Arab towns and villages. My thanks to all those people who simply went about their lives without regard for us observers from another time. Without such support and encouragement, this book and much else I have come to value in recent months would, I fear, have remained unthought and unwritten.

Finally, this preface must be burdened with a rather long apology for the language in which some of the interpretation is presented. Raymond E. Brown (*The Community of the Beloved Disciple*, p. 131) has observed that today one would prefer to use his/her; brother/sister and so on, but that the Johannine letters constantly refer to "brothers." Rather than distort the situation, he has chosen to go ahead and speak of "brotherly" love in the letters. We have felt the same discomfort in preparing this commentary and have decided to accept the same solution. The reader who wishes to see what other resources the Johannine tradition has for understanding the role of women should consult Raymond Brown's masterful discussion of that theme (*Community*: 183-98).

However, those resources are not reflected in the Johannine letters. Elsewhere in christianity the love command is phrased as "loving one's neighbor"; in the fourth gospel as "loving one another," an expression which also occurs in the letters. "Brother" as the designation for christians only appears twice in the gospel: in the risen Jesus' command to Mary (20:13) where it refers to Peter and the disciples, and in the account of the beloved disciple's death (21:13), a passage written by a disciple of the evangelist, perhaps even the author of the Johannine letters. In the letters, the situation is quite different. Not only is "brothers" a standard way to refer to christians (1 Jn 3:13; 5:16; 3 Jn 3,5,10); it is employed in many of the formulations of the love command (1 Jn 2:9,10,11; 3:10,14,15,16,17; 4:20,21). Contrast this situation with the ethical exhortation in Jas 2:14-16, for example. Though that author addresses his audience as "brothers," the deeds by which they show their faith are helping a "brother or sister" in need. 1 Jn 2:12-14 ties the more general Johannine self-designation "children" together with "fathers" and "young men."

We suspect that this preference for "brothers" is no accident but derives from the fact that the parties involved in the disputes which occasioned these writings were men. Both the false teachers and the author's missionary associates are "brethren." Contrast that situation with the condemnation of a woman as a false prophet and teacher in Rev 2:10-23. Undoubtedly the paraenetic tradition on which the author drew, especially that derived from baptismal catechesis, to remind his audience of what they had heard "from the beginning" had been addressed to both men and women. But the author clearly conceives his audience as men. Male missionaries, leaders and teachers are the ones involved in thrashing out the problems about which these letters are speaking. Therefore, in retaining masculine pronouns and expressions like "love the brothers," we merely reflect the particular context of the exhortation in the Johannine letters. (The reader should be reminded that "fellowship" translates a greek word, *koinonia*, which does not indicate a group of a particular sex.) We have no way of knowing the extent to which, if at all, women were involved in these discussions.

Holy Week, 1979

INTRODUCTION

Why Read the Johannine Letters?

WHEN ASKED what is the New Testament, most people can come up with the gospels, maybe Acts, the major Pauline letters, maybe Hebrews and Revelation, but the ten smaller letters, of which 1-3 John are a distinct group, are almost never mentioned. The few who do mention them usually have no idea what they are about. Though not as theologically exciting as the major New Testament writings, these letters do have a fascination of their own. They let us into the world of early christian communities struggling to establish themselves as part of the larger graeco-roman world. We always need to be reminded of how very small christianity was during its first century. Many christian claims reveal their astonishing, even revolutionary, character only when we get beyond our picture of christianity, the world religion, back to the "grass roots" origins of the movement. It is just those "grass roots" that we recover when we read the small, less known writings in the New Testament like the Johannine letters.

However, we hasten to add that the "grass roots" are not without their own insights and genuine developments of christian spirit and understanding. For example, "God is love," a statement many would regard as the greatest insight and foundation of devotional christianity, appears here in 1 Jn 4; not in the gospels or letters of Paul—though there is much in their universally shared conviction of God's unremitting care for his creation to found such a conclusion. 1 Jn also insists that a person must believe in Jesus, a flesh and blood person, as revelation of God's love and must belong to the community which is to embody that love, if one is to be saved. Most christians would agree that his convictions represent ideals of christian belief and practice. In 1 Jn, we have the opportunity to see how these ideals came to be expressed in a concrete situation; how they were understood to be at the foundation of christian community. Then we can enter into our own dialogue with the author: how do his insights challenge contemporary christian reflection?

The Authorship and Context of the Johannine Letters

Since these writings are traditionally referred to as 1-3 John, one might assume that they are by the author of the Gospel of John. But, if you read them through quickly, you will see that they never make such a claim for themselves. The author is only claiming the authority of a teacher who knows what the testimony to Jesus "from the beginning" has been. He never appeals to what he has written before. (Unlike Luke at the beginning of Acts or Paul in 2 Cor, for example.) Yet we cannot say that the letters were written before the gospel. Look carefully through the Gospel of John and you will see that it focuses on problems created for the community by jewish opponents, who have expelled christians from the synagogue communities (Jn 16:1-4a). They are insisting that it is blasphemous to speak of Jesus as Son of the Father (see the debate in Jn 8). The Johannine letters, on the other hand, describe problems of internal strife, not external persecution. No one is denying the divinity of Jesus; but some christians are accused of denying his coming "in the flesh" (see 1 Jn 4:2). Judaism is not mentioned. 1 Jn 5:21 warns christians to beware of idols. The majority of the community would now seem to be pagan converts rather than former jews.

But, if the letters are not by the author of the gospel, (see one of the scholarly commentaries for linguistic arguments to support this conclusion), then the author must

still have been close to the evangelist. 1 Jn uses many
symbols and expressions from his work. Since many interpreters of the gospel think that a disciple gave it its final
form after the evangelist had died—adding some of the
latter's preaching and explaining his death—, this disciple
might even have been the author of the letters. Part of the
change in focus between the gospel and the letters shows
that christians now have to articulate for themselves what
they believe. They are not responding to the external pres-
sures and arguments of jews or jewish christians as in the
gospel. Most interpreters agree that even the views opposed
by the author of 1-2 Jn were developed as interpretations
of the fourth gospel's picture of Jesus. But these views were
not merely theological speculation for its own sake, they
were creating serious problems for the community. Relationships between christians have become strained (2-3 Jn).
Many scholars like to think of 1 Jn as the first commentary
on, perhaps even better, the first pastoral application
of the gospel.

Because he is writing to a specific group of communities,
"churches," all of which belong to the Johannine tradition,
the author leaves us with many questions. He does not need
to explain in detail the views he is opposing. He can just
allude to them or perhaps, parody some of his opponents'
favorite expressions. There are also passages in 1 Jn which
look as though they are independent sections. Perhaps they
are examples of the kind of paraenesis, (ethical exhortation),
that was frequently used in Johannine churches. The author
can then make his case for true christian tradition by
referring to them. We can sometimes guess that a passage
derives from such traditional preaching, when we find that
its form or content is like christian preaching from non-
johannine traditions found in other parts of the New
Testament or in early christian writings. We will be asking
you to look at such passages elsewhere in the New Testament as we go along. But often, we find ourselves in the
position of having to guess what the opponents might have
been saying, and sometimes the information given is not
sufficient for us to be sure.

Three kinds of external evidence can also help us to understand the Johannine communities better. First, thanks to archaeology, the study of ancient inscriptions, and the thousands of private and public letters, documents, and writings that have survived on papyri in Egypt, historians know more and more about how people lived and related to one another at this time. They also help clarify our picture of the religious ideas held and the religious associations formed by inhabitants of the cities of the eastern part of the empire. Thus, we have a better picture of what people expected of each other and their gods.

Secondly, the Dead Sea Scrolls, writings of the jewish Essenes found at Qumran, continue to yield a wealth of information about the organization, beliefs and practices of a first century jewish community. Although there is no evidence to support the claim that christianity derived from the essene sect, their writings have shown us examples of scriptural interpretation, community organization, and theological language about God, humanity and the impending end of the world, which illuminate many facets of the New Testament. These comparisons suggest that the Scrolls and the New Testament traditions independently reflect religious beliefs and practices common across a broad spectrum of 1st century judaism. Even when the Gospel of John was written, sometime around A.D. 90, christians found their exclusion from the wider jewish community painful. Some people may even have preferred to remain jewish rather than to publicly admit their belief in Jesus as messiah (cf. Jn 12:42f). We may assume, then, that the parallels to essene language and perhaps community rule became part of the tradition of the Johannine community during its period of close association with judaism. They form part of the past tradition which the author wants his audience to recall as he assesses new claims about Jesus and christian salvation. We will see that he takes a similar stance toward some traditional christian formulae.

Although written later than the Johannine letters, newly published gnostic writings from Nag Hammadi (in Egypt) can help us understand some of the ideas the opponents seem to have been trying out. Comparisons between 1 Jn and patristic accounts of the gnostics had long ago suggested to people that the author's opponents might have been christians whose theology had taken a gnostic turn. They are clearly not gnostics in the sense of the 2nd century christian gnostics. There is not even the slightest hint that they would deny that the Father of Jesus and the creator god are one and the same, as 2nd century gnostics regularly do. Nor, as far as we can tell, have the opponents carried speculation about the nature of Jesus as revealer to the lengths that 2nd century gnostic interpreters of the fourth gospel would do. But the piety of these opponents and their rejection of a sacrificial interpretation of the death of Jesus certainly find a home in later gnostic tradition. The new writings give us examples of the gnostics' explanations of Jesus, their ideal of community, and their own polemic against orthodox christianity. They help us correct many false ideas about gnosticism which are still being used to interpret statements in the Johannine writings, and the traditions reflected in the christian gnostic writings themselves provide further clues as to what these opponents might have been saying.

Finally, we would agree with many interpreters who point out that the problems reflected in the Johannine letters are a microcosm of the process any religious community must go through as it tries to consolidate what it has gained from the past—its teaching, its ritual, its image of the founder, its ideal of community—in the face of the future and the changing socio-religious context of its members. It must find new interpretations of that past and new forms of internal organization.

Literary Characteristics of the Letters

Although we commonly refer to all three writings as "letters," they represent three different literary genres. 1 Jn is not a letter at all, but an instructional tract which may have been intended to be circulated among several communities. 2 Jn is a letter to a community or group of communities which are different from that in which the author usually lives, but close enough for him to suggest that he may visit them. 3 Jn is a private letter to a friend, Gaius, who lives in yet another community. Both 2 & 3 Jn are like the private letters that survive on papyrus, but also have features in common with the christian letter form as we know it from the Pauline correspondence.

Before turning to the individual writings, a brief description of the author's method of composition may help you read them. See how many examples of the various features you can come up with yourself.

Some scholars have attempted to isolate a written source, which the author then rewrote in composing 1 Jn. However, there does not seem to be enough stylistic and linguistic evidence to support reconstruction of such an independent source. We shall also argue that such a method of sticking together texts is unlike the author's tendency toward allusion and oral composition. Instead of supposing that the author has revised some text, we think that he has a variety of sources at his disposal, most of them oral in character. He appeals to a number of traditional formulae. Some of them derive from christian tradition older than the fourth gospel. The fourth gospel, itself, seems to draw on synoptic-like traditions about Jesus, which may have circulated freely in the Johannine church. Other allusions to synoptic-like tradition in 1 Jn probably derive from the same source (cp. for example, 1 Jn 3:7//Mk 13:5, and Mt 5:48; 1 Jn 5:3//Mt 11:30). The author treats the fourth gospel in the same fashion. He does not quote it as we would but alludes to it. (1 Jn 1:4=Jn 15:11; 1 Jn 3:11=Jn 15:12 come closer to being direct quotations, but they may have been used as formulae in the community.) Some of the slogans the author uses to distinguish true christian belief from false seem to have been formulated during the controversy with the jews at the time the gospel was written. Confession that "Jesus is messiah (christ)" or "son of God" was a badge of christian allegiance and willingness to suffer persecution. 1 Jn is using the old slogan in a new situation where christians are divided among themselves. Jewish accusations against christian belief are no longer an issue; he does not appeal to the Old Testament. (Brown, *Community*, 134, thinks that 1 Jn 2:11 may be an application of Is 6:10 from Jn 12:39f to the opponents. If so, it is a very distant allusion to Isaiah indeed.)

Modern commentators are often puzzled by the author's failure to appeal to scriptural authority—especially to that of the fourth gospel. They would sometimes have us believe that the author does not appeal to the Gospel of John because his opponents have made a strong case for their own view by using it. Therefore, the author is compelled to find oblique modes of argument and to only make general appeals to tradition. Such arguments reflect a typical modern misunderstanding of the oral modes of cognition and authority which were still very much part of the world of the 1st and 2nd centuries. Texts achieve a status as canonical authority in a context in which most people have adopted literacy with the ensuing switch to abstract modes of cognition as the primary means of knowing truth. The educated upper class, schooled in philosophy, might have made that shift, but most people, even those who had had enough education to be able to read, had not done so. For them, real knowledge still derived from the oral world of direct, face-to-face, communication. When the New Testament was canonized as a sacred scripture as a result of the 2nd century struggles with heresy, an important cognitive and religious shift occurs in christianity: it becomes possible for the foundation of true faith to be associated with the interpretation of a sacred text. We must be careful not to read the results of this shift back into the time of the Johannine letters. Many interpreters make this mistake when they envisage the members of the Johannine circle as a "school" manipulating texts or interpreting the fourth gospel as though it had the status of sacred text. For Johannine christians such texts only had life as they were read aloud (remember most people in antiquity did not read silently even to themselves), that is, they were returned to being "word" in the oral sense. As such, those words had no more or less authority than other words spoken solemnly within the community—as part of a liturgical celebration, say, or as preaching. Another example of the priority of face-to-face communication can be found in the formula which concludes both 2 & 3 Jn: the author has not written everything because he hopes to visit and communicate with the addressee directly. Usually misinterpreted as the kind of promise of a visit someone in our society might make, this expression seeks to invest the inferior mode of writing with something of the superior face-to-face communication that can only take place orally.

We also find the priority of oral cognition reflected in the composition of 1 Jn. Oral discourse is formulaic and repetitive—or so it seems to us, who are accustomed to the direct, analytic and logically formulated arguments made possible by literacy and especially by print media. You can always reread this page or look up passages to which I refer. As a writer, I can refer back to all sorts of books, xeroxed articles, notes and outlines, and even, now that the whole book has been through several drafts, to what I am going to say later on. Without these tools, the whole character of our exchange would be different. The theme-and-variations approach of 1 Jn with its citation of tradition and well-known confessions of faith and perhaps liturgical tradition, would play an important role, since they could be relied on to trigger and "stay with" our common memory. 1 Jn refers to that memory when he keeps reminding his audience of what they have heard "from the beginning." In cultures with no written documents at all, the common memory is the custodian of all information, technical skills, social arrangements, legal agreements, and religious traditions. The community *is the witness.* Although it was no longer necessary for all important information to be committed to common memory, the feeling for the relationship between community and tradition in the Johannine letters is saturated with the presuppositions of oral understanding. The author of 1 Jn may even allude to preaching he himself has done within the community (e.g. 1 Jn 2:15-17; 3:11-24; 4:19-5:3). He has taken up accepted phrases and slogans—some of them may have been popular with his opponents—and modified them to provide an acceptable version. Such modifications are common in oral composition. With such things as print, xerox, and home video cassettes, we require a high degree of correlation between one account and the next before we will say that the two are identical. Studies of oral cultures, on the other hand, indicate that two accounts are considered identical if 50-60% of the words are the same. Thus it is possible for a story or tradition to undergo modification or even be updated to fit the environment of its hearers without its being regarded as "changed." Even after the advent of writing, identity had a much looser definition than we would be inclined to give it today. Therefore, we must be careful not to suppose that the changes against which the author protests were based on the kind of verbal nuances which we would consider to be alterations of the tradition; they had to be substantively out of phase with the tradition. We cannot even be sure that all members of the community would have reacted in the same way as the author did to the new preaching; perhaps to them it sounded identical.

Other commonly observed features of the author's style also fit into the oral context. He constructs sentences that are almost formulaic parallels using conditional clauses, "if x . . ." or the definite article (sometimes followed by the Greek word for everyone) and a participle, usually translated into English, "everyone who" (cp. 1 Jn 1:6,8,10; 2:4,6,9). In the same contexts you can also find another favorite device, antithetic parallelism, stating the same thing positively and then negatively (also see 4:7f). In other places, there are genuine antitheses (1 Jn 3:7-10; 4:4-6; 5:18f; 3 Jn 11). Such devices belong to a rhetorical tendency to repeat the same thought with variations in expression.

New sections pick up the concluding words of the previous section. The end of a section may return to a word or words from the beginning as an *inclusio*. Associative links between words and thoughts—not logical syllogisms—provide the movement from one sentence to the next. The net effect of the whole, then, is of a spiral motion of return to a slightly different formulation of what we began with; not of the direct forward march of analytic argument.

We have dwelt at length on the oral character of the author's composition because it is the most foreign to our own ways of understanding and analysis. Failure to appreciate it leads commentators to treat 1 Jn and his opponents as though they used and related to texts in the same way as we do. They have even drawn such unwarranted conclusions as the claim that he did not know the fourth gospel as we have it, since he does not cite it as an authority. We will see that he is constantly citing the gospel by what we would describe as allusion. Such a mode of citation was probably as good as quotation, however. Some people have even claimed that the author was backed into a corner by his opponents' interpretation of the gospel and cannot appeal to it. Actually, his evocation of the common memory and testimony is not the weak argument of a person lacking textual support—as it would be today—but the strongest possible appeal within the context of orally constituted tradition and authority. The testimony of the community is what really counts.

Scholars who are not sensitive to the language of oral cultures often misinterpret statements about opponents in ancient writings. You would get the impression from reading some modern interpreters of the Johannine letters that the community was being violently ripped apart by the debates to which the author refers. One must remember that the institutionalization of orality in an educational system based on rhetoric fosters a kind of polemic stance and hostile language quite unlike anything we are used to. Personal attack, boasting, and challenges were all part of the on-going fabric of life. We do not have to go back to antiquity to see how different our expectations are. Read—or better listen to—recordings of old political debates before television and video tape could freeze the candidates' words and beam them around the globe. Then look at a modern television debate. The former is much more personal, "hostile," and also more exciting. The passions and moral sensibilities of the audience are roused in a way that rarely happens when a person knows that everything he or she says will be frozen and replayed on thousands of nightly news broadcasts and analyzed to death on panel discussions. Now imagine a world in which that experience of personal, oral debate is common fare. No value is placed on our standard of impartial objectivity. The point of rhetoric was to use every means possible to see that one's own position, the true or good one, prevailed over its "bad" opposition. Even sciences and medicine were discussed in terms of *conflicts between forces*, of battles that had to be won. Everything would be colored with the value to be attached to it, good or bad, for or against. There is no neutral observer. I stress this point because we will be talking constantly about the author's opponents. Remember that "opposition" is the norm for discussion in a rhetorical climate. Failure to appreciate the difference between oral culture and its rhetoric and our own "detached" language can lead a modern reader to overestimate the severity of the problem. When the author speaks of his opponents having broken fellowship with his community, we perhaps have to think of the various types of feud and breaking off of association that occur in close knit oral societies. Such a dispute may only involve close friends or families. Though discussed as an irrevocable break, it may not have the permanency we would associate with that language. (Blood feuds or those deriving from serious personal injury or injury to property are different from the everyday feuds that derived from opposition of ideas, loyalties, or slighted honor or dignity.) Such disputes do not destroy the whole fabric of a community. Most communities have various forms of social pressure against the potentially destructive effects of their own polemical use of language. Several hours after the most dire exchange of insults and threats the opponents may be going about their business as though they had never fought. Bearing these characteristics of face-to-face society in mind, we must not jump to sweeping conclusions about the ecclesiological consequences of the debates we are about to witness in the Johannine letters. We must always temper our own strongly negative reactions to the hostile language ancient authors use in describing their opponents. The gnostic writings give examples of sweeping condemnations of orthodox church authorities; while gnostic christians, at the same time, admit to living within the christian communities, run by those same authorities. Their language has frequently been hypostasized by modern scholars into an elaborate anti-institutional theory and rebellion curiously out of harmony with the lack of evidence for independent forms of social organization. So too in the Johannine case. Although the author refers to his opponents as having separated from his community, there is no indication that they have really set up an opposition church. Thus, we must insist on a less polemicized reading of 1-3 Jn than is currently in fashion.

ONE JOHN

THE FOUNDATION
OF TRUE CHRISTIAN
FELLOWSHIP

Outline

1 JN IS A TREATISE for the instruction of christians in the community; not a personal letter. Since the author relies on repetition, variations on a theme, and word associations, it is difficult to divide the writing into clearly bounded sections. Certain images and metaphors are unevenly distributed throughout the work and may provide some clues. The image of light and darkness as ways of life only occurs up to 2:11. Following 2:29, that image seems to have been replaced by the metaphor of the christian as the one "born from God." Similarly, 2:23-5:12 keep returning to the theme of possessing God and Christ. "Believing" appears in 3:23 to be picked up again in 5:1-13. Chapter 4 has alternative formulations of these themes which focus on doctrine and "confessing Jesus," both of which first emerge as issues after 2:23. The author tends to repeat and to overlap themes so that deciding on precise verse divisions is more difficult than recognizing the major sections. It seems clear that there are divisions around 2:11; 2:28 or 29; 3:23 or 24; and 5:12 or 13, with 5:14-21 as an additional appendix. (Some scholars even attribute it to a different hand.)

3

Since it is so difficult to arrive at a precise outline on the basis of content or literary features, a common approach has been to outline 1 Jn in terms of alternating ethical and christological sections, though it remains difficult to separate the two. The following outline from Schnackenburg's commentary is typical of the approach. He himself admits that it does not solve all the problems of the epistle and he uses somewhat different divisions for the commentary itself (p.10).

> Prologue 1:1-4
> A. Ethical 1:5-2:17, walking in light as the sign of true community with God.
>   Christological 2:18-27, belief in Jesus as the foundation of true community with God.
> B. Ethical 2:28-3:24, doing righteousness as the sign that one is "born from God."
>   Christological 4:1-6, the Spirit from God acknowledges Jesus Christ in the flesh.
> C. Both are tied together
>   4:7-21, love as the foundation of faith.
>   5:1-12, faith as the foundation of love.
>   Conclusion 5:13-21.

The third section of 1 Jn is least amenable to this analysis.

You may also have noticed that in terms of space ethical concerns far outweigh doctrinal ones. Commentators have tended to devote equal space to christological considerations, but it is not at all clear that they are the real cause of the problem. Christological slogans may be used as part of a polemic which centers around a breach whose real roots are in christian praxis. The dominant issue is christian fellowship—as will also turn out to be the case in different ways in 2 & 3 Jn. The unity which the Johannine gospel had idealized in response to the earlier crisis of expulsion from the synagogue once again finds itself strained. 1 Jn seems intended to be a "rule" for the community life of those who follow the teaching of "the elder." Ethics, not christology, is the author's concern throughout. We suggest the following outline. The commentary on the individual sections will explain our choice of divisions and the problems still inherent in it:

Prologue 1:1-4, remain in fellowship with us.
A. Ethical: Two Ways Paraenesis 1:5-2:17
B. Conflict: Do not be Deceived by the Antichrists 2:18-29.
> vv.28-29 on confidence in the judgment are transitional; they conclude this section and introduce the next.
C. Ethical: Reformulation of "A" 3:1-24
> vv.19-24 are a concluding summary which emphasizes christian confidence before God.
D. Community Rules 4:1-5:12
> 4:1-6, antichrists require testing of the spirits (cp. 2:18-27)
> 4:7-16a, love in the christian community (cp. 3:1-18)
> 4:16b-21, "God is love" (cp. 1:5) as the basis for confidence in the judgment (cp. 2:28-29)
> 5:1-12, "Jesus is the Christ" as the basis for being a child of God; for confidence in the judgment and in eternal life (cp. 3:19-24)
> Conclusion 5:13 (cp. Jn 20:30)
> Appendix 5:14-21, rules for prayer and community discipline. (The theme of confidence in judgment occurs here in association with prayer.)

Community Rule and the Crisis of Confidence

After the first section, which is likely to have been based on traditional baptismal paraenesis, the work has a recurring motif of confidence in relation to the judgment and other eschatological rewards such as eternal life. We know from the essene writings as well as from New Testament passages like Mk 13 that sectarian apocalyptic communities viewed division as a sign of the end-time. This motif is repeated in 1 Jn 4:1-6. Such groups insist, of course, that the unity and religious purity of their community insures that they will survive the coming judgment. Lack of this certainty about their salvation seems to be troubling members of 1 Jn's community; they are not sure of their own status with regard to judgment or eternal life. What would cause such a crisis? Certainly the opponents cannot have been the moral libertines which some readers of 1 Jn have taken them to be—though the author never accuses them of any explicit lapses in morality. They would seem to be serious christians; perhaps even advocates of a higher degree of moral purity than that common in the community.

Both the gnostic and essene materials provide us with examples of such perfectionism. The essenes insisted that none of the ritual purifications prescribed in the Law would benefit a person who was not purified by strict observance of all the precepts of the Law as interpreted in their tradition. Other, non-observant Jews would find themselves condemned along with the gentiles in the coming judgment. The gnostics, far from being the moral libertines they were often accused of being, often show concern for a strict ascetic practice which would free the soul from the passions and desires that it derives from association with the body. The soul cannot ascend to its heavenly home unless its ties with the evil, material world are broken. They often claim that christian baptism is useless; true perfection must be attained by freeing one's soul from passion and attachment to the things of this world. 1 Jn cites perfectionist slogans derived from his opponents, though, like any rhetorician of the time, he tries to insinuate that those who hold such a view must be amoral, must consider themselves incapable of sinning. Since we have no evidence of a group which held such views, we must take them for what they are: a rhetorical attempt to discredit one's opponent.

The anxiety that seems to have been engendered by the "perfectionist" preaching of the opponents may have been intensified by the Johannine tradition itself. The gospel presents the sum total of Jesus' ethical teaching in the command to "love one another"—a tradition continued in the paraenesis of 1 Jn. If the opponents held up as the only true standard of perfection either a christian *halachah* on the analogy with judaism or an ascetic perfection of a "passionless" soul on the analogy with gnosticism and the pagan philosophical praxis from which gnostics derived their view, then the Johannine christians could well have become anxious about their status in the judgment because they lacked any standard for measurement to hold up against these other claims. 1 Jn seeks to deal with their concern by explaining that the love of God shown in Jesus is the true foundation of their community and source of Christian sinlessness. He continues to hold up the love commandment as the one norm of behavior and relationship to God.

REMAIN IN FELLOWSHIP WITH US.
1:1-4.

> **1** That which was from the beginning, which we have heard, which we have seen with our eyes, which we have looked upon and touched with our hands, concerning the word of life—²the life was made manifest, and we saw it, and testify to it, and proclaim to you the eternal life which was with the Father and was made manifest to us—³that which we have seen and heard we proclaim also to you, so that you may have fellowship with us; and our fellowship is with the Father and with his Son Jesus Christ. ⁴And we are writing this that our joy may be complete.

The introduction to 1 Jn is an excellent example of how those accustomed to oral tradition weave together a fabric of familiar allusions rather than use the direct quotations and appeal to authority that we expect. The language of the fourth gospel pervades the section, since it clearly stands at the foundation of the community's discourse. Obvious parallels to the prologue of the gospel are found in the images of beginning, word and life in the presence of God. There these metaphors characterized the word of God about to be made manifest in a hostile world. Here, the author of 1 Jn looks back on that manifestation as the foundation of the christian community, which he is hoping to hold together by his exhortation.

Metaphors from elsewhere in the gospel also occur in this section. Unless we pick them up, we miss the full impact of what the author is saying. The expression "from the beginning" appears in two different contexts in the gospel. It can refer to the testimony to be given by the disciples, who are Jesus' witnesses "from the beginning" (Jn 15:27). In Jn 15:11 Jesus tells his disciples that he has spoken with them so that "their joy may be full" (cf. 16:20-24; 17:13). You can see from 1 Jn 1:4 that the author has framed the introduction by allusion to these two passages. His audience is to be sure that his and their joy will be full just as Jesus has promised.

"From the beginning" also appears in a negative context. In Jn 8:44 it designates the true nature of the opposition to Jesus: the devil is a liar "from the beginning." 1 Jn 3:8 picks up that passage from the gospel. The devil is a sinner "from the beginning," and Jesus has appeared (= "made manifest" of v.2) to destroy his works. The expression "made manifest" in v.2 often occurs in the gospel in association with the works of Jesus showing the Father to those who have faith to see Jesus' true identity (Jn 2:11; 9:3; 7:4, in reference to an inappropriate demand for such a showing; 17:6, Jesus has "made manifest" the Father's name to the disciples). Or, it may refer to human actions whose true nature is "made manifest" by the appearance of Jesus as light (3:21). Similar usage is found in 1 Jn. "Made manifest" can refer to Jesus' coming as savior (1 Jn 3:5,8). Or, it can refer to the distinction between people that is now at issue: the true children of God who remain in fellowship with the author and the tradition "from the beginning" as opposed to those who have departed from their community (2:19, 28; 3:10).

Emphasis on the "appearing" of Jesus represents an important theological development made by the Johannine tradition. Pauline theology stresses the death and resurrection of Jesus as the saving event. The Johannine tradition has not lost that traditional interpretation of the death of Jesus (cf. Jn 12:46; 1 Jn 4:9,14; 5:6); but it has broadened the concept of saving event to include the whole life of Jesus—the power of eternal, divine life has come into the cosmos (1 Jn 2:17 ; see Schnackenburg: 62f). The saving significance of Jesus' coming from the Father is not reduced to any part of his activity. It is not simply bringing revelation about God—a reduction popular among gnostics for whom the death of Jesus has no relation to our salvation; it is merely the unfortunate consequence of the hostility of the evil powers who rule the world to the coming of revelation. Nor is it simply a sacrificial death and resurrection as in the Pauline tradition, which runs the risk of making the life of Jesus insignificant except in how it ended.

The tradition of testimony about what has happened in Jesus becomes especially important in christian communities in which most or all members have not known either Jesus or any of the original disciples. The fourth gospel concludes with a benediction for those who have believed without seeing (20:29). Jn 17:20-23 gives these later christians the same mission of testimony and the same glory, unity and love with Father and Son that was bestowed on the original disciples (see Perkins: 197-205). The fourth gospel makes it clear that later christians stand in the same relation to Jesus and the Father as the first disciples because of the presence of Jesus in the testimony of the community and the eucharist, a presence which is not caught in the limits of historical time (Perkins: 241f). 1 Jn does not want christians to lose sight of the fact that everything they now experience as coming from Jesus depends on their continuing in continuity with him as he was made manifest to those first witnesses. Remember, when the author of 1 Jn speaks about what is seen and touched, he is not referring to the kind of facts about Jesus we would have if people had been able to videotape his life and hand the tapes on to us. The gospel makes it clear that many people who saw and heard Jesus, even those who witnessed his miracles, did not become believers (e.g. 2:22f). They did not see that he was from God. Only those who could see Jesus' works as manifesting the glory of God would become witnesses to him (2:11).

Commentators frequently assume that the language about "seeing, hearing and touching" Jesus was directed against gnostics who denied the reality of Jesus. That approach flounders on the fact that gnostics never deny that Jesus has a body which can be seen, handled and touched. A 2nd century gnostic work, the *Gospel of Truth* (GTr) even alludes to this passage from 1 Jn in support of the gnostic preaching about Jesus (CG I *3* 30,27-31,20; *NHLE*: 43f). (See Bibliography: Robinson.) Joy characterizes the gnostic reception of salvation. They are encouraged to bear witness to the truth about Jesus. And, finally, the Father's love for them makes gnostics true brothers and children of the Father (43,5-24; *NHLE* 49). But the gnostics also claim that Jesus brought a new revelation about the Father, which was not known before and which is only attainable to those who are gnostics. Sometimes, they insist that Jesus did not reveal the true nature of the Father or his own glory to the disciples until after the resurrection. Everything reported about the earthly life and teaching of Jesus would have to be interpreted in the light of that esoteric revelation. 1 Jn seems to be using the language of "seeing, hearing and touching" to evoke personal presence and to establish the claim that only their tradition derives from that presence. In the Johannine tradition, there is no break between the earthly and risen Jesus or between Jesus and what the community came to understand about him through the spirit (e.g. Jn 14:26; 16:13).

The Johannine tradition is famous for its expressions of the unity of believers with each other and with the Father and Son. When John speaks about God or Jesus dwelling "in" the believer, he is not referring to some private, individual inner divine presence. He always uses that language when speaking about the community of believers that has been brought into being by Jesus' "appearing." Nor does he restrict realization of divine presence to religiously gifted individuals—mystics or people of outstanding holiness. It is shared equally by all who belong to the community, since for John the only real locus of light, truth, glory, life, and spirit from God is Jesus himself. These are not aspects of the divine which any individual might discover within him or herself. Thus the issue of christian fellowship is crucial. There is no other place of eternal life. Conflict within the community threatens to rupture the unity on which the tradition sets such store. You can see that theme throughout chapters 15 and 17 of the gospel, the chapters to which the author has alluded in his opening appeal. Unity with Father and Son and mutual love are the hallmarks of that new community. The author wishes to recall to his audience the basis of their fellowship.

The word *koinonia*, fellowship, only occurs here (v.4) and in the introduction to the next section (vv.6f). Otherwise, the author uses more characteristically Johannine expressions. Perhaps, he has chosen the word as a headline to emphasize the problem or perhaps it was used by his opponents. The author will go on to recall the true roots of any such fellowship. The most characteristic Johannine expression is "remain or abide in." Throughout the gospel remaining in or with Jesus is used to mean staying with him as disciple rather than being led to reject him by the jewish opposition (e.g. 15:4; Perkins: 173). That way of speaking can easily be carried over into this new situation in which some christians seem to form a separate group and to encourage other members of Johannine communities to follow their lead. Two aspects of discipleship are associated with expressions of "remaining or abiding": sticking with the teaching about Jesus (1 Jn 2:24,27f; 2 Jn 9), and leading a life appropriate to a believer, one of mutual love (2:6; 3:6; 4:12). 1 Jn uses the related expression "to be in God" in a similar way (2:5; 5:20). Sometimes he varies the metaphor by speaking of abiding in an attribute of the Father: truth (1:8; 2:4); his word (1:10; 2:14); his seed (3:9); eternal life (3:15); love (4:12). The carefully constructed allusions to the fourth gospel in this section stress the fact that the fellowship shared by the author and his audience is grounded in Jesus, himself. Fellowship is not some elective choice about doctrine or community organization.

WALKING IN THE LIGHT.
1:5-2:17.

The first major section of 1 Jn presents fellowship as remaining in the community in which there is true forgiveness of sin. Remaining in that community implies love for its members. The language of this section: dualistic contrast between light and darkness as ways of life; concern with the ethical purity of the community, and allusion to the final judgment of God, fits a pattern of jewish and early christian ethical preaching known as "two ways." Perhaps the best known jewish example is found in the community rule from Qumran. You will notice that the community rule plays an important part in identifying the member of the group. Members are exhorted to love their brethren, the "sons of light," and to hate outsiders, "the sons of darkness," (1 QS 1.9f). 1 QS 3.13-4.26 contain two ways teaching under the head of the two spirits which struggle for humanity's allegiance. Notice that the final destruction of sinfulness, the spirit of perversity, is associated with the cleansing action of the spirit of God, which is compared to the ritual waters of purification (4.19-23). Gal 5:17-24, a short christian example, show the features common to such exhortation: (1) dualistic introduction, spirit/flesh (vv.17f); (2) double catalogue of virtues and vices (vv.19-21a,22f); (3) eschatological reference (21b,24). Other early christian examples are found in the Apostolic Fathers, *Barnabas* 18.1-21.9 and *Didache* 1.1-6.2. If you compare these, you will notice that in *Didache* the concern with light and darkness and angelic powers characteristic of 1 QS and *Barnabas* has been replaced by the metaphors of life and death. You will also notice that the later christian authors have used teaching of Jesus from the synoptic tradition as an important component of the content of their paraenesis. Baptism and confession of sin still appear in the context of "two ways" exhortation, thus suggesting that its original context was the initiation of new members into the community. The Qumran example is clearly associated with the initiation ritual, which also required confession of sinfulness by the members (1 QS 1.24f; also CD 20:28b). Here in 1 Jn 1:8-10, we find confession of sinfulness as part of the exhortation to "walk in light." The dualistic division between members of the community and outsiders who "walk in darkness," suggests that this Johannine exhortation also derives from an initiatory context. It defined the initiate as set apart, as a member of those saved by the coming of Jesus.

Though one cannot accept Bultmann's reconstruction of a source document behind this part of 1 Jn (Bultmann: 18), the insight that the author is using material from another context does seem correct. 1 Jn is referring back to preaching which his audience knows from another context, probably their initiation into the Johannine community. Throughout this writing, the author wishes to distinguish christian fellowship from the common kind of private religious association in which people from a particular country or trade might join together to honor some patron deity. Membership in such clubs was a matter of social choice, though one might have strong reasons for joining a particular group and leaving it might be interpreted as an act of "hatred." Such groups might often split if a particular cult became popular. Groups of people from different countries might also have independent associations for the worship of the same deity within one city. We would not be too surprised if some members of the Johannine community took a similar attitude toward their own association. The author wishes to appeal to the language of christian initiation in such a way as to make casual dividing of that fellowship impossible. A person who does not remain within it cannot have forgiveness of sin and righteousness from God.

This emphasis is enhanced by the peculiarity of Johannine "two ways" exhortation. Although there are general references to commandments in the plural (e.g. 1 Jn 2:3f; cp. Jn 15:10), only one commandment is ever stated, love the brethren (2:7). The Johannine gospel has a similar movement. Commandments in the plural are mentioned; but only the love command is explicitly given as such (Jn 15:10-12; also 13:34 and 14:15,21). It is clear that the Johannine tradition understands love as the defining characteristic of its community. In the gospel, this "love one another" is emphasized in the face of external hostility and persecution, which threatens to break up the community and has caused some members to leave. These memories from the past were well-engrained in the language and memories of later christians, who had not lived through them, by the repetition of the gospel stories. 1 Jn can now invoke them to address the new situation in which people are leaving as a result of internal division rather than external persecution.

1:5 God is Light

> ⁵This is the message we have heard from him and proclaim to you, that God is light and in him is no darkness at all.

The section begins with an appeal to an accepted metaphor for God, light. The image of the divine as light was widespread in both hellenistic pagan and jewish piety. The word translated "message," *angelia*, may be the Johannine equivalent of the more familiar Pauline "gospel," *euangelion* (Brown: 108 n. 214). It reappears in 3:11 where the *angelia* heard from the beginning is the love command. After the prologue to the work, we might have expected "message" to have been followed by "from the beginning" rather than the somewhat vague "from him." "From him" is probably intended to be equivalent to the expression "from the beginning" and to indicate that what the author is about to present is in continuity with what has come from Jesus through the testimony in the community. It could not indicate an allusion to the teaching of Jesus, since the metaphor appears neither in the synoptic tradition nor in the fourth gospel. The latter, in fact, stresses Jesus as light of the world. It uses light as symbol of his saving presence (Jn 1:4,5,9; 8:12; 9:5; 14:9).

1 Jn typically focuses on God the Father where the gospel might have emphasized Jesus as revelation of the Father. 1 Jn uses titles for Jesus which belong to christian tradition earlier than the gospel and which might have been applied to any righteous person (cf. 1 Jn 2:7f) without evoking the charges of blasphemous identification of a human being with God raised in the gospel. Jesus is messiah (2:22), son (1:3; 3:23), sin-offering (1:7; 2:2; 4:10), and advocate (2:1). This treatment of Jesus has led some interpreters to suggest that 1 Jn was written before the gospel and the development of its christology. However, allusions to the gospel in 1 Jn and the reflection of the gospel's christology in the language of dwelling with Father and Son lead us to reject that view. Instead, 1 Jn shows us that it was possible to have a picture of Jesus' divinity such as is presented in the fourth gospel without eclipsing the Father's place in christian life and reflection. All too many christians today identify Jesus with God in such a way that they do worship only one God, Jesus. 1 Jn does not fall into the

kind of di-theism claimed by the jewish opponents of christianity in the gospel controversies. If anything, the powerfully sketched picture of Jesus in the gospel had revitalized confidence that God was active for the salvation of those who trusted in him. When applied to Jesus in the gospel, light imagery symbolized his revelation as saving humanity. Applied to the Father, here, it symbolizes the perfection and purity of his divinity. But unlike many forms of hellenistic and gnostic piety, association of light with divine being did not mean that people were to seek a personal, private, interior vision of that divine light. It meant, as the author will go on to spell out, that they were to conduct their lives in obedience and fidelity to the community which that God had acted to establish (1:6f; 2:10f).

1:6-10 Fellowship of Those who Walk in the Light

> [6] If we say we have fellowship with him while we walk in darkness, we lie and do not live according to the truth; [7] but if we walk in the light, as he is in the light, we have fellowship with one another, and the blood of Jesus his Son cleanses us from all sin. [8] If we say we have no sin, we deceive ourselves, and the truth is not in us. [9] If we confess our sins, he is faithful and just, and will forgive our sins and cleanse us from all unrighteousness. [10] If we say we have not sinned, we make him a liar, and his word is not in us.

This string of conditional sentences is a fine example of the author's use of antithetical parallelism. Statements of erroneous views, "if we say that . . . ," and their consequences alternate with presentation of the true action of christians, walking in the light, confession of sinfulness, and the resulting fellowship and forgiveness. Just as the whole section was introduced by a statement characterizing divine being, "God is light," so each statement about true christian action is associated with another attribute of God himself. He is "in the light" (v.7; = "is light" v.5), and he is "faithful" and "just" (v.9; cf. Exod 34:6f; Dt 32:4). Verse 10 concludes the section and forms an *inclusio* with v.6.

We saw that the initiatory setting of two ways paraenesis in both judaism and early christianity included confession of sin. The essene neophyte is about to be cleansed (1 QS 1.16; 3:12; CD 20:28f) by entry into the community of the elect. Christian tradition has always associated baptism with forgiveness of sins (Mk 1:5; Mt 3:6). 1 Pet 2:9b speaks of the new convert from paganism as one called out of darkness into the light of God. And Eph 5:8-13 encourages christians not to associate with any kind of immorality by referring back to their baptism as coming from darkness into the light given by Christ. They are exhorted to "walk as children of light" (8b; cp. 1 Jn 1:7a). These parallels clearly indicate that 1 Jn is recalling the baptismal paraenesis of his community.

Early christians went beyond associating forgiveness with baptism to claim that forgiveness of sin was effected by the death of Jesus. Originally, the idea that the death of Jesus was a sacrifice for sin may have originated in the gentile mission. The gentiles who had been living lives totally separated from God (the darkness of Eph and 1 Pet) and without access to the means of salvation and atonement he had given the jewish people in the Law, now had a sacrifice to atone for their sins. Paul (Rom 3:21-25) expands such a tradition to present Jesus as the sin-offering for all christians both jews and gentiles. The gentiles need his gift of righteousness because of their long history of turning away from God; the jews because they have constantly been disobedient and broken the covenant God had made with them. So now God has provided all of humanity with a new righteousness, one which does not make any distinction between jew and gentile (see also Rom 5:8-11; Eph 1:7; Col 1:20-22; and similar expressions in non-Pauline writings, Heb 1:3; 9:12; 1 Pet 1:19). 1 Cor 15:3 shows that by the 50s A.D. the death of Christ "for sins" was a standard part of christian belief (as does its formulaic use in epistolary introductions like Gal 1:4 and 1 Pet 1:2). The fourth gospel did not exploit the image of the death of Jesus as sacrifice however. There Jesus lays down his life as part of a plan by which that death is his exaltation and return to the glory he had with the Father. However, the sacrificial interpretation is mentioned. Reference to Jesus as "lamb of God" 1:29 recalls other early christian sacrificial interpretations (e.g. Heb 9:2; 1 Pet 1:19; Rev 7:4). Jn 11:50 refers to the death of Jesus "for the people" as making possible the incorporation of the gentiles into the people of God. Therefore, such language about the death of Jesus was probably always part of the paraenesis of the community.

The "word of God" negated by refusal to acknowledge the need for cleansing from sin effected by Christ (v.10) does not refer to the pre-existent word, but to God's word of promise. The positive teaching about forgiveness in this passage is clear enough. One would also expect the exhortation to a new life of holiness such as that in v.6 (cp. the paraenesis in Eph 5:8-13). When people misinterpreted the "freedom from sin" granted in baptism to mean that Christians were free to do anything they chose, New Testament authors always reminded them that their conduct had to correspond to the new reality given in baptism. But they do not go to the extent that the essene community does in trying to embody perfect holiness and purity in the community through a high standard of obedience to the Law; careful ranking of members; punishments for infractions (cf. 1 QS 1.24-26; 6.24-7.25). Even the essene admits that real purification from sin is not within the realm of mere human achievement but must depend upon the eschatological gift of the spirit of God.

The puzzle in this section lies in the false claims of sinlessness reported in vv. 8 and 10. Nothing in the context suggests that members of the Johannine community were following a libertine interpretation of christianity such as may have been the case among some of Paul's gentile converts. Therefore, we should probably not interpret these verses to mean that the author's opponents were asserting that it was impossible for a christian to commit sin. Such charges were sometimes made against gnostics.

The evidence of our gnostic writings, however, suggests that the problem might have been a claim to perfection based on moral and ascetic seriousness; a seriousness which led to denial of a divine forgiveness mediated by baptism or the sacrificial death of Jesus. Such writings insist that each person must achieve perfection through his or her knowledge and ascetic practice. One must conquer the passions of the soul and become free from attachment to the material world or the body. Several late 2nd century or 3rd century gnostic texts explicitly attack the orthodox claim that the death of Jesus atones for sin. A tract which preaches severe asceticism as the way to salvation, *Testimony of Truth*, says that any God who would demand a human sacrifice would be vain-glorious, and could not be the true God (CG IX *3* 33,19-21; *NHLE*: 408). Another, less concerned with asceticism than with gnostic survival in the face of christian persecution, attacks the orthodox for thinking that they can be saved and become pure by "cleaving to the name of a dead man" (*Apocalypse of Peter* CG VII *3* 70,10-15; *NHLE*: 341). These examples make it clear that it was possible to reject the association of forgiveness of sins with the death of Jesus out of a concern for moral perfection and asceticism. Such a claim did not imply moral laxity or the claim that gnostics cannot sin no matter what they do. Since the fourth gospel had not emphasized sacrificial imagery in depicting the death of Jesus, it would have been easy for members of the Johannine community to claim that their quest for perfection was in line with the traditional picture of a Jesus who is free from the passions and snares of the world. The author of 1 Jn seems to have caricatured their position by implying that it was a claim to present and past sinlessness.

2:1-2 Jesus our Advocate

2 My little children, I am writing this to you so that you may not sin; but if any one does sin, we have an advocate with the Father, Jesus Christ the righteous; [2]and he is the expiation for our sins, and not for ours only but also for the sins of the whole world.

1 Jn now turns from the application of baptismal paraenesis against his opponents to address his audience. The
expression "little children," first used here, will become
common (2:12,28; 3:7,18; 4:4; 5:21). In wisdom literature,
the address "my son" or "my child" indicates the teacher/
pupil relationship between the sage and those he is instructing. The phrase "little children" occurs once in the
fourth gospel at the beginning of the farewell discourses.
Jesus uses it when he turns to address his true disciples
after the betrayer has gone out (13:33). In the next verse he
introduces the commandment of love for one another
(13:34). Thus, 1 Jn is able to evoke the solemn context of
Jesus' final legacy to his faithful disciples by using this
instruction. He will shortly remind them specifically of
the love command.

The baptized christian should not sin, but if he does,
the author assures him that Jesus stands as his heavenly
advocate. This approach is quite different from the elaborate rules about loss of food, table fellowship, community
rank, and temporary or permanent exclusion from the
community which the essenes used to deal with the sins of
those who had entered its new covenant.

Jesus as Advocate

The expression "advocate" or *paraclete* only occurs here
and in the fourth gospel. The sayings about the paraclete in
chapters 14-16 of the gospel show a complex history of
development. Johannine use of the term may have first
come into play during controversy with the jews. One can
find in almost every sector of judaism the belief that Moses
will intercede for his people before God just as he had done
on earth. Jn 5:45 attacks that confidence by claiming that
Moses is on the side of Jesus. He will not intercede for the
jews who reject Jesus but will turn and accuse them. Jesus
is consistently portrayed as greater than Moses (Jn 1:17f)
so it is not surprising that he should take on the function
of heavenly advocate as well.

Just as was the case with christological titles, the picture of the paraclete in the gospel is more complex than 1 Jn's appeal to Jesus as heavenly advocate. There, the paraclete stands almost as an independent figure whose activity is associated with the life of the community in the world rather than with the heavenly presence of Jesus at God's right hand. In Jn 16, the paraclete fulfils the functions that a more traditional eschatology expected of the Son of Man's glorious return in judgment. Those who have rejected Jesus stand condemned (16:7-10), and christians learn that all the messianic prophecies have been fulfilled in Jesus (16:13). In Jn 15:26, like the spirit in the synoptic tradition, the paraclete assists christians who must testify to their faith in Jesus. In chapter 14, the image of the paraclete seems to be convertible with the in-dwelling language that expresses the presence of Father and Son to the community (see Perkins: 189-96). The polemic formulations of chapters 15 & 16 are clearly not relevant to the situation in 1 Jn, and the author prefers the indwelling expressions for divine presence. Many commentators assume that the author is basing his teaching on the experience of the paraclete in the community without realizing that "paraclete" was not a fixed figure in Johannine language but a fluid symbol which could take on different functions in different contexts. 1 Jn suggests that the community commonly spoke of Jesus as the heavenly paraclete.

Jesus can be conceived as a heavenly advocate like Moses without associating that function with his death for sins. 1 Jn insists that it is precisely his death for the sin of the world which underlies his present intercession for the community. A similar image of Jesus occurs in the letter to the Hebrews. The exalted Jesus, who made the perfect sacrifice for sins in his death, now intercedes in heaven (Heb 7:25-27). Thus, the Johannine picture of Jesus as advocate has appropriated the larger picture of Jesus' atoning death. "World" in v.2 is not a symbol of all that is hostile to God as it is in 2:15-17 but simply refers to all of

humanity (as in Jn 1:29; 3:16f; 4:42; 12:47). Bultmann
thinks that the addition of advocacy as part of Jesus'
atonement for sin was a late development. Later gnostic
evidence shows that they could accept the picture of Jesus
as heavenly advocate for sin (*Apocryphon of James* CG I 2
11,4-6; *NHLE*: 34) without an associated doctrine of the
death of Jesus as atonement. This particular gnostic writing
makes extensive use of Johannine traditions apparently in
response to orthodox polemic against the gnostics. If you
read it, you will notice that the discussion of sin which
follows on the assertion that Jesus will be heavenly inter-
cessor depends upon an anthropology of spirit—soul—
body. A soul filled with the spirit will be able to keep the
body from sin; the body itself is not an object of salvation.
Jesus' prayers may attain forgiveness for the gnostic, but the
real victory over sin is not achieved by such intercession.
It must be won in the individual spirit—soul. 1 Jn, on the
other hand, has no such anthropological analysis. Jesus'
intercession and atoning death make forgiveness a permanent reality within the community. That forgiveness is
experienced any time the christian falls short of the perfection which he or she seeks.

2:3-6 Keep his Commandments

> ³And by this we may be sure that we know him, if we
> keep his commandments. ⁴He who says, "I know him" but
> disobeys his commandments is a liar, and the truth is not
> in him; ⁵but whoever keeps his word, in him truly love
> for God is perfected. By this we may be sure that we are in
> him: ⁶he who says he abides in him ought to walk in the
> same way in which he walked.

The author goes on to exhort his audience not to sin.
The presence of forgiveness in the community is not a license
to let up on one's efforts to "keep his commandments." The
expression "I have known him (= God)" in v.4 has led many

interpreters to assume that the author's opponents claimed a direct vision or knowledge of God as the goal of religious perfection; a vision which negated concern for ethical behavior in the community. Such a caricature of gnostic piety hardly suits the evidence. Gnostics do accuse the orthodox of a false claim to knowledge of God and truth because they (the orthodox) fail to recognize the revelation of the true God in Jesus (cf. ApocryJas CG I *2* 9,24-10,5; *NHLE*: 33). If the expression "I have known him" is a slogan of the author's opponents, one should interpret it along the line of Schnackenburg's suggestion (p. 99) that the crucial difference in revelation between the two sides is focused by 1 Jn's insistence that *Jesus was sent by the Father to make atonement for sin in the flesh.* For a gnostic, such a claim could never express the truth about God and Jesus or about sin.

However, we favor an alternate hypothesis that the expression "I have known God" was not a slogan of the opponents but one that had developed within the Johannine tradition. Jesus says to Thomas in Jn 14:7: "If you had known me, you would have known my Father also; henceforth you know him and you have seen him." We suggest that the expression "ones who know God" came to be used to characterize the knowledge of God belonging to the members of the Johannine community during its conflict with judaism and does not refer to any particular doctrine of the present opponents. In this section, the author is reformulating the baptismal paraenesis of 1:5-7. The return to the expression "walk" in v.6 refers back to that section.

Further allusions to the farewell discourses broaden the imagery of the treatise and prepare for the introduction of the new commandment in vv. 7-11. Verse 5 assures us that the love of God is perfected in the person who keeps his (= Jesus') word (cf. Jn 8:51f; 14:23f). The RSV has translated the genitive expression "love of God" as "love for God" as though it referred to human love directed toward God. Most interpreters disagree. The genitive does not refer to the object of the love but to its subject, that is, to God as the one who loves humanity (cf. 1 Jn 4:8,16,20; 5:2f), which is the usual usage in the Johannine tradition. Further support for that interpretation may be derived from the farewell discourses. We suggest that this verse is an alternative formulation of the indwelling language of Jn 14:23f: "If someone loves me, he will keep my word, and my Father will love him, and we will come and make our home with him." The individual's love is directed toward Jesus in keeping his word, and toward other christians. For the Johannine tradition, the perfection of God's love for humanity is attained in the community of those among whom the Father and Son dwell.

The concluding verse of the section appeals to Jesus' "walking" as an example for the christian life. The expression "abide in" while equivalent to the "be in" of the previous verse very often carries overtones of adversity: one remains a disciple of Jesus despite hostility or external pressure. The allusion to Jesus' example may be intended to recall Jesus' own appeal to his example in the footwashing story (Jn 13:15). That story is particularly apt in this context, since the gospel uses it as the preparation for Jesus' commissioning his true disciples to take over the task of bearing testimony, of being the "ones sent by Jesus" (13:16,20).

2:7-11 The New Commandment

> 7Beloved, I am writing you no new commandment, but an old commandment which you had from the beginning; the old commandment is the word which you have heard. 8Yet I am writing you a new commandment, which is true in him and in you, because the darkness is passing away and the true light is already shining. 9He who says he is in the light and hates his brother is in the darkness still. 10He who loves his brother abides in the light, and in it there is no cause for stumbling. 11But he who hates his brother is in the darkness and walks in the darkness, and does not know where he is going, because the darkness has blinded his eyes.

All the allusions to the farewell discourses now break out into a clear reference to Jesus' commandment of love as the characteristic of his community. At the same time, that "new" commandment is also part of the testimony to which the tradition has witnessed "from the beginning." It is the epitome of Johannine paraenesis. "From the beginning" carries overtones from 1:1 of being part of the tradition from Jesus, but its more immediate reference is to the beginning of the audience's own instruction as christians. The author is still recalling their baptismal paraenesis. "Beloved" seems to have been a common form of address in early christianity (1 Jn 3:2,21; 4:1,7,11: 2 Jn 2,5,11; cp. Rom 12:19; 2 Cor 7:1). Those who hold that the entire section is aimed directly at the opponents suggest that the author is speaking of the commandment as "old" to distinguish it from the doctrinal innovations of the gnosticizing group (cp. 2 Jn 9). We think that the author is not yet speaking about his opponents but is using baptismal paraenesis to establish a common ground between himself and his audience as required by the rhetorical tradition. "Old" emphasizes the importance of Jesus' "new" commandment (Jn 13:34) as the foundation of the community. The next verse turns to the "newness" of that commandment: it represents the fulfilment of the eschatological promise of light. Early christian preaching frequently spoke of the life of christians being lived in light, light which was to be fully realized at Jesus' return. They could live in that light because the darkness of a sinful world was already passing away. We have seen this use of "light" in our discussion of Eph 5:8-14 (see above on 1 Jn 1:6-10). You can also find it in 1 Thess 5:4-10 and Rom 13:11f.

Some gnostic ascetics took over this language of apocalyptic paraenesis. In *Thomas the Contender*, for example, Jesus the revealer is the true light which shines to call people out of the "world of bestiality," away from the flesh and sufferings and passions of the body, into union with him (CG II 7 139,31-140,5; 145,8-15; *NHLE*: 190; 194). 1 Jn, of course, has no such ascetic interpretation of the symbol.

Rather than continuing his earlier reference to God as light, 1 Jn seems to have shifted to the gospel's image of Jesus as the light of the believer in the world (Jn 8:12; 9:5; 12:46). Verses 9-11 refer to Jesus' claim to be the light in which the believer abides, and also to a simile used for his presence in the world at Jn 11:9: the person who walks by day does not stumble; he who walks at night does because he does not have light *in himself.* The RSV has obscured this allusion by opting to translate the *en auto* of v.10b as "in it" rather than "in himself" though they note the other possibilty. Their translation gives a smoother reading to v.10b but hides the allusion. Verse 11 combines this reference with another saying about Jesus as light from Jn 12:35: the one who walks in darkness "does not know where he is going." Such combinations are a common feature of oral preaching and teaching such as the author has been using throughout.

The real exegetical difficulty in these verses is understanding the negative formulation of the love commandment as a prohibition against "hating one's brother." The only references to hatred in the fourth gospel are to that directed at christians from the outside (as also in 1 Jn 3:13). The community rule at Qumran does instruct people to love the members of the sect and hate outsiders (1 QS 1.2f; 9.16, 21f), but such expressions are not paralleled in the New Testament. The usual meaning of "brother" in the New Testament is "fellow christian," which also seems to be the meaning of the injunction to "love one another" in the Johannine formulation of the love command (Jn 13:34; 15:12-17), since only Jesus' friends, the circle of those he has just purified (13:10) receive the teaching. (Also see the "love one another/the brethren" in 1 Jn 3:11,13,15,23; 4:7,11,12,20f; 2 Jn 5). But some commentators think that 1 Jn may have a wider context of christian love—perhaps the injunction to love one's enemies—in mind. They point to 1 Jn 4:21 where the combination of love of God and brother could be a Johannine translation of the double command of love of God and neighbor. Thus, they would like to see this teaching as a reference to love of neighbor which is not limited to the christian community.

But the issue is far from clear. 1 Jn 3:17 speaks of the necessity of helping a brother in need in a context which even those who favor a wider interpretation of the love command admit must refer to christians. Jas 2:14-17 shows that such paraenesis was common in early christian preaching. In order to understand what is involved in this teaching, we must remember that the needs of the poor were dealt with through socially established networks of family, trade associations (often provided for one's burial), or attachment to a rich man as patron. Jews embodied the Old Testament teaching of care for the poor among their people by dispensing charity through the synagogue. You can see that it would be necessary for christians to come up with their own forms of social support for members whose conversion left them without the traditional means of assistance. The Johannine community as a whole may have been forced to focus on "love for one another" in a special way during the persecution at the time the gospel was written. One common form of such early christian "love for one another" was hospitality. Missionaries and other christians who had to travel sought the hospitality of churches in the cities to which they went. Travelers in the ancient world would commonly seek out the area of a city where people from their home country had settled—perhaps organized around worship of a native deity, or trade association, or in the case of Jews a local synagogue. 3 Jn deals with a crisis caused by a failure to respond to such a request for hospitality. For a member of the christian community, helping a fellow christian in need might well require that he or she associate with persons whom race, class, or trade might normally incline one to avoid or dislike. We can see from Paul's problems at Corinth that it was very easy for christian communities to break up into social groups based on traditional loyalties. Thus, it seems to us that 1 Jn is consistently using the love command to refer to fellow christians, and that this command had achieved its prominent place in the community during the period of persecution when members lost their traditional support (as in the story of Jn 9). However, in the social context of these Johannine Christians the requirement to love one's fellow christian in the same way that traditional loyalties demanded one treat a member of one's family had the same broadening effect of the general injunction to love one's enemies—or that demands that christians be concerned for the suffering and oppressed no matter who they are have today. A person had to go beyond some very strong traditional loyalties to family, friends, social class, trade, etc. to meet the demands of this new community. The command to "love one another" is not a case of retreating from the wider "love your enemies" into a world of those with whom one is familiar and comfortable as it might be today.

2:12-14 The Victory You have Won

> [12]I am writing to you, little children, because your sins are forgiven for his sake. [13]I am writing you, fathers, because you know him who is from the beginning. I am writing to you, young men, because you have overcome the evil one. I write to you, children, because you know the Father. [14]I write to you, fathers, because you know him who is from the beginning. I write to you, young men, because you are strong, and the word of God abides in you, and you have overcome the evil one.

The author breaks into chant-like formulae to remind his audience that they are not among those walking in darkness because they have conquered sinfulness through the forgiveness received in Jesus. The expressions "father, young men, children" link this section with a common literary form in early christian preaching, the "household code." In such "codes," the preacher would set out the duties of each class of people in the congregation in turn (e.g. Eph 5:22-6:9; Col 3:18-4:1). The earlier part of the

Ephesian material has already provided parallels to the use of "two ways" in 1 Jn. Since that "two ways" paraenesis is followed by a household code, we suspect that the author has chosen his style of speaking because such a code was part of the traditional paraenesis of the Johannine community as well. But he does not, in fact, set out a table of duties. Instead, he once again invokes the language of the fourth gospel to assure his readers that they have won the promised victory through their faith. His aim seems to be to bring the audience to a conviction of the superiority of their faith before he turns to deal directly with the threats to it in 2:18.

Verse 12 addresses all believers. They have received forgiveness both through baptism and through their continued presence in the community as the author has already explained. The RSV rendering of the phrase which says literally "for the sake of his name" as "for his sake" obscures the author's allusion to Jn 1:12: those who believe in his name are children of God (cf. 3:18). None of the attempts by exegetes to attach the remaining terms to specific groups or officials within the community (i.e. fathers=elders) has won much support. It seems that the various designations derive from the literary form the author is using, while the content of the victory described could be applied to any member of the community. "Knowing the one from the beginning" (vv. 13a; 14b) refers to Jesus, though the author maintains the close association between knowing Jesus and knowing the Father (v. 14a) from Jn 14:7-10. We have seen that Johannine christians probably came to term themselves "those who know God" during the controversy with the jews (cf. above on 2:4). The assertion of victory over the Evil One directly recalls Jesus' claim to have conquered and cast out the ruler of this world (Jn 12:31; 16:33; cf. 1 Jn 3:13; 5:18). We know from passages like Eph 6:12 that christian preachers used the imagery of the christian protected by faith in the war against the Evil One. 1 Jn may also have in mind Jesus' prayer that the Father protect from the Evil One those whom he is leaving in the world (Jn 17:15; cp. 2 Thess 3:3). Verse 14c gives the basis for victory in that context of "armour of faith," namely, "you are strong." In a typically Johannine turn, what would be the armour of faith in traditional preaching becomes "keeping the word of Jesus" (cf. 1 Jn 2:5). 1 Jn 5:4 tells us that everyone born of God conquers the world. Thus, we must assume that in this passage the author has taken the titles from the traditional household code to provide a rhetorical variation in his assurance to the community that their faith in Jesus has won forgiveness, knowledge of God, and victory over evil—just as they have always heard in Johannine preaching.

2:15-17 The World is Passing Away

> [15]Do not love the world or the things in the world. If any one loves the world, love for the Father is not in him. [16]For all that is in the world, the lust of the flesh and the lust of the eyes and the pride of life, is not of the Father but is of the world. [17]And the world passes away, and the lust of it; but he who does the will of God abides for ever.

Allusion to the impending destruction of this world is characteristic of two ways paraenesis. By recalling that traditional language, the author both concludes the opening exhortation and provides a transition to his claim that the opponents are "antichrists," heralds of the end-time in 2:18. The expression "the world is passing away" appears in the context of apocalyptic paraenesis in 1 Cor 7:31. There Paul encourages christians to avoid entanglement in marital relationships because the end of the world is so near, "the form of the world is passing away." The association of the transitory character of the world with desire (RSV "lust") indicates that such apocalyptic paraenesis was the source of the tradition reflected in vv. 16-17. But 1 Jn never focuses on the *nearness* of the end. Rather, the transitory character of the world stands in contrast to the eternity of the one who does the will of God. That contrast calls to mind the contrast, in Wisd 2-5, between the righteous who live forever with God and sinners who perish. "Do the will of God" is a traditional expression in jewish and christian preaching. The more usual Johannine translation of that occurs in the language about love for the Father in v.15. If you look at Eph 5:11-16 again, you will notice that after the exhortation to "walk in the light" christians are told to be sure and have no part in the world of darkness. The same progression connects this passage to the previous one. After assuring his audience that they have won the eschatological victory, they are exhorted not to love the world, Eph vv.15-16 also tone down the language about the nearness of the end that had characterized apocalyptic paraenesis. The warning to watch how one lives is placed in the more general context of the present as "evil times." Such an expression would originally have referred to the evil of the days just before the end of the world. Now it is used as a more general characterization of the world in which people live, just as 1 Jn is using the apocalyptic expression about the transitory nature of the world to contrast it with God and the righteous person.

The mini vice-list in v.16 defines what love for the world is. Opposition to desire/lust appears frequently in both christian and gnostic paraenesis. "Lust of the flesh" appears in Eph 2:3 (cp. "fleshly desires" in 1 Pet 2:11; Did 1:4, both from baptismal paraenesis). Mt 5:28 might be adduced as an example of the connection between desire understood in the sexual sense and the eyes. However, we also find a saying in Wisd 14:9 which connects the eyes with greed. The final member of the chain "pride of life" explicitly refers to the boasting of a person who possesses wealth. *Bios*, translated "life" here, refers to worldly possessions (cf. 1 Jn 3:17; Mk 12:44). There is a long section of christian preaching against the passions and "friendship with the world as enmity with

God" in *James* 4. It is our closest New Testament example of the kind of preaching 1 Jn 2:16-17 is summarizing. Jas 5:1-7 uses eschatological language to undergird its presentation of the transitory nature of worldly wealth and pleasure. In James "pride/arrogance" refers to the boasting of a wealthy person. We can understand the concerns of this type of christian preaching better if we remember that in the roman world *ostentatious consumption* was the rule rather than the exception. Rich people made sure that everyone knew how much superior they were by their rich dress, haughty speech, by being carried through the streets in fancy litters followed by crowds of attendants, by having large numbers of clients waiting outside their houses, by following a rigidly hierarchical order in seating people at banquets and seeing to it that any guests of lower station were constantly reminded of the fact since they were treated with contempt by the slaves and served worse food than nobler guests. No one was allowed to forget for a minute how he stood in relation to such a person of wealth and power. This type of behavior is the "pride of life" or arrogance being castigated in 1 Jn 2:16 and in the more lengthly attack on the wealthy in James. Thus, we conclude that the mini-catalogue in 1 Jn refers to three types of behavior: "lust of the flesh" to all the physical passions, not just sexual desire (note that Jas 4:1-3 ties greed as the cause of war with the desire to indulge physical passions); "lust of the eyes" refers to greed; and "pride of life" refers to the arrogant behavior characteristic of the rich and powerful.

We have seen that the language of apocalyptic paraenesis passed into gnostic circles as the complete condemnation of the body and the material world as the source of desires which trap the spirit and keep it from returning to its true divine home. Freedom from desire required rigid disciplining of the body. Some scholars have seen this passage in 1 Jn as a reflection of that gnostic mentality. We cannot agree, since it clearly stems from the tradition of baptismal paraenesis in a community which also stressed the permanent availability of forgiveness for those seeking perfection. However, such traditions of ethical preaching were easily given an anti-worldly ascetic interpretation as the gnostic evidence shows. They may have been used by 1 Jn's opponents to support their own claims for an ascetic perfection among christians.

DO NOT BE DECEIVED BY THE ANTICHRISTS 2:18-29.

[18]Children, it is the last hour; and as you have heard that antichrist is coming, so now many antichrists have come; therefore we know that it is the last hour. [19]They went out from us, but they were not of us; for if they had been of us, they would have continued with us; but they went out, that it might be plain that they all are not of us. [20]But you have been anointed by the Holy One, and you all know. [21]I write to you, not because you do not know the truth, but because you know it, and know that no lie is of the truth. [22]Who is the liar but he who denies that Jesus is the Christ? This is the antichrist, he who denies the Father and the Son. [23]No one who denies the Son has the Father. He who confesses the Son has the Father also. [24]Let what you heard from the beginning abide in you. If what you heard from the beginning abides in you, then you will abide in the Son and in the Father. [25]And this is what he has promised us, eternal life.

[26]I write this to you about those who would deceive you; [27]but the anointing which you received from him abides in you, and you have no need that any one should teach you; as his anointing teaches you about everything, and is true, and is no lie, just as it has taught you, abide in him.

[28]And now, little children, abide in him, so that when he appears we may have confidence and not shrink from him in shame at his coming. [29]If you know that he is righteous, you may be sure that every one who does right is born of him.

Having established the community of believers on the basis of traditional exhortation, 1 Jn confronts the challenge threatening to divide the christian community. He begins by invoking the apocalyptic image of the antichrist, the final manifestation of evil in the last days (Mk 13:21-23, "false christs and prophets"; 2 Thess 2:3-12, the man of lawlessness, cf. Dan 11:31; Rev 13, the beast from the sea). In the usual apocalyptic scenario, such figures are cosmic or political in scope and lead people into sin or pagan belief with false signs. The author of 1 Jn assumes that his readers are familiar with the image, and he suddenly applies it in the plural to the christian opponents who are leading people away from the traditional teaching. Notice that there are no "signs and wonders" associated with the people to whom he is referring. In this respect 1 Jn is quite unusual. Even when the same imagery is used in gnostic texts of the 2nd century, it still retains the traditional cluster of associations. *Paraphrase of Shem* predicts the coming of a demonic figure (given the use of ancient near eastern water-monster mythology this figure is closest to Rev 13), who will lead people away from the true gnosis (CG VII *1* 43,28-45,31; *NHLE*: 326f). Gnostics can even epitomize their suppression by orthodox authorities by speaking of an end-time in which a false god, complete with signs and wonders, will arise and pervert the teaching of the gospel (*Concept of Our Great Power* CG VI *4* 44,13-46,5; *NHLE*: 288). 1 Jn makes no attempt to impose that sort of cosmic imagery on the group he is opposing. Therefore, we do not accept the claim made by some interpreters that his use of "antichrist" shows his eschatology to be more primitive than that of the fourth evangelist. As in the previous passage, he simply takes over apocalyptic language to intensify the picture of the seriousness of the opposition; he is not interested in apocalyptic preaching about the impending end. Note, for example, he does not go on to predict the apocalyptic destruction of his opponents, something even the later gnostic writings do!

Verse 19 makes it clear that the people in question were not new converts but established members of the community. It is also clear that their separation was not the result of a formal excommunication such as we know was the penalty for severe lapses from the essene rule and was prescribed by Paul in a severe case of immorality (1 Cor 5:3-5). The author's concern to assure his audience that these people are not really "from us" (v.19c) and to warn them against being led astray by their teaching (v.26) shows that they have not established a completely independent sect. Rather, like many later gnostics, they considered themselves christians and continued propagandizing within the christian community.

However, this section does not make clear the nature of their teaching. Commentators have tried to find forms of gnostic christology to fit v.22 "deny Jesus is the Christ." But while it is true that many gnostic christologies distinguish the heavenly, spiritual part of the revealer, the immortal man, Son, or Son of Man, from his bodily part, they do so in order to free the divine from any involvement with sinfulness, suffering or death. They frequently give explanations of the virgin birth of Jesus in order to show him as a worthy vessel for the divine spirit (cf. *Tripartite Tractate* CG I *5* 115,3-116,30, *NHLE*: 87f, here even the apostles have a special origin; *Gospel of Philip* CG II *3* 55, 23-36; 71,13-15, *NHLE*: 134; 143; *Second Apocalypse of James* CG V *4* 50,8-51,13, *NHLE*: 251; *Testimony of Truth* CG IX *3* 30,18-31,5, *NHLE*: 407, in this ascetic work Jesus must be pure and undefiled by passions). The heavenly revealer may even take the crucified Jesus up to his dwelling with the Father (*Trimorphic Protennoia* CG XIII *1* 50,12-15, *NHLE*: 470). There is no known gnostic christology that really fits the slogan. We suggest that v.22 never was intended to represent the opposing point of view. The language of vv.22-23 is very close to that which emerged from the polemic with judaism in which the distinctive theological language of the Johannine gospel developed. At that time, people were denying the messiahship of Jesus, and much of the controversy swirled around the Johannine insight that the Son is the only true revelation of the Father. The gospel continuously insists that no one can claim to

accept or believe in God—as the jewish teachers did—
without accepting Jesus (5:23; 8:19; 12:44f; 14:9; 15:23;
16:3; 17:3). As any good rhetorician might do, our author
is assimilating the present crisis to the symbols developed
in the past one in which many of the members of the community had suffered persecution (15:23; 16:3, the persecution is associated with the slogan of the identity of Son
and Father). His opponents would certainly reject any
connection with those who had denied Christ rather than
suffer persecution. But the author knows that if he can
appeal to the loyalties formed during that crucial period
in the community's history through using its slogans, he
will have marshalled opinion to his side.

We have already mentioned that the symbol of the
paraclete developed as part of the authority of christian
claims for Jesus when pitted against jewish opposition
(see above on 2:1f). Jn 14 shows paraclete language to be
convertible with that about the spirit and the indwelling
of Father and Son. 1 Jn is evoking these images. It is likely
that spirit or anointing was the more usual way of speaking
about the activity of the divine within the community. As
in the gospel, possession of the spirit belongs to the whole
community. 1 Jn does not develop a doctrine of some spirit-
endowed official within the community to hand on and
safeguard the tradition. The spirit as anointing guides the
community as a whole to faithful witness to the teaching
"from the beginning." We have already suggested (see
above on 1:1-4) that such a picture of the community fits the
pattern of oral tradition very well. Some commentators
think that he has picked the term "anointing" in opposition
to its use among gnostics, but it was more likely the way in
which Johannine christians commonly supported their
claims to true religious insight (vv.20f; 26f). It may also
have had associations with baptismal initiation. Just as the
paraclete in Jn 14 is to lead the community to true understanding of Jesus' teaching and may be considered identical
with the indwelling Father and Son (Jn 14:16f; 26), so 1 Jn

is convinced that testimony to what has been from the beginning within the community anointed by the spirit, or alternatively, the community which remains in unity with Father and Son, is sufficient to counter false teaching.

The apocalyptic language of v.18 returns in vv.28-29. The author has constructed his initial response to the opponents in two parallel sections vv.20-25//26-29. Both begin by asserting the effectiveness of testimony within the "anointed" community against false teaching, and then conclude with an eschatological promise to those who *remain in* that community. (For this reason, we have not followed the practice of most commentators and attached vv.28-29 to the beginning of chapter 3, although the re-formulated tradition in v.29 does seem to have been designed as a bridge to the next section of the epistle.) Verse 25 uses typically Johannine language to promise the believer eternal life. Like v.18, vv.28f return to apocalyptic images. The faithful believer can be confident that he or she will not be shamed at the judgment (v.28). Verse 29 takes a traditional assertion, the righteousness of God demands that one do righteousness to be saved and casts it in Johannine language, the one who does righteousness is born of God. The expression "born of God" provides a bridge to the next section, which will return to ethical instruction. Apocalyptic paraenesis always considered ethical not doctrinal statements as the norm for the coming judgment. It may be that the opponents had been arguing that Johannine christians were not sinless enough (ascetic enough?) in their praxis to survive judgment or gain eternal life—a criticism which seems to have shaken the confidence of the community.

THE CHILDREN OF GOD.
3:1-10.

> **3** See what love the Father has given us, that we should be called children of God; and so we are. The reason why the world does not know us is that it did not know him.

²Beloved, we are God's children now; it does not yet appear what we shall be, but we know that when he appears we shall be like him, for we shall see him as he is. ³And every one who thus hopes in him purifies himself as he is pure.

⁴Every one who commits sin is guilty of lawlessness; sin is lawlessness. ⁵You know that he appeared to take away sins, and in him there is no sin. ⁶No one who abides in him sins; no one who sins has either seen him or known him. ⁷Little children, let no one deceive you. He who does right is righteous, as he is righteous. ⁸He who commits sin is of the devil; for the devil has sinned from the beginning. The reason the Son of God appeared was to destroy the works of the devil. ⁹No one born of God commits sin; for God's nature abides in him, and he cannot sin because he is born of God. ¹⁰By this it may be seen who are the children of God, and who are the children of the devil; whoever does not do right is not of God, nor he who does not love his brother.

1 Jn 2:29 provided the transition to this section by speaking of those who do righteousness as God is righteous as being "born of God" and confident of their salvation. Chapter 3 picks up these themes. The children of God are distinguished from the children of the devil. Then, at the end of the chapter, it returns to the confidence possessed by the community in which the spirit of God dwells. This section provides some of the basis for that confidence, since the christian community possesses righteousness and sinlessness. There is little that is new in this section of 1 Jn. The author picks up the themes of traditional paraenesis to reinforce the conviction and allegiance of the members of his audience. He seeks to lay bare the essential distinction between them and the opponents whom he wishes to show are "not of us." As in the previous section, one method of making this distinction is to allude to the language of the gospel in such a way as to identify the present opponents with those of the gospel.

The expression "children of God" seems to have been one of the community's traditional self-designations. Perhaps they had moved away from the more common "sons of God" when that expression came to be used to refer to the unique relationship between Jesus and the Father. The expression "children" occurs in close proximity with another favorite, "born of God," which Jn 3:5 suggests was associated with baptismal initiation into the community (cf. born in 1 Jn 2:29; 3:9; 5:1; 5:18; children in 3:1,2,10; 5:2). Judaism had already developed the image of the righteous person as "son of God." It occurs in Wisd 2:18 and 5:5, a passage which we have already connected with Johannine paraenesis in 2:16f. The righteousness brought by Jesus led christians to claim to be "sons of God." Rom 8:12-25 may well represent the kind of christian preaching that we find here cast into Johannine language. Romans uses both "children" and "sons" for the new status of christians. That status derives from the fact that the spirit of God enables christians to live a new life "not according to the flesh"; to address God as Father, and to hope and long for the future revelation of glory in which they will receive full adoption as sons of God. 1 Jn is without the cosmic imagery of a transformed creation—unless one reads "dissolving the works of the devil" in those terms. But the passage expresses similar sentiments. Christians stand in a special relationship to God now as a result of what Christ has already done; they live a renewed life which is not subject to sin, but at the same time, the salvation which he has made possible is not completed in the present. Christians still hope for the future conformity to Christ and for the revelation of his true glory—which for the Johannine tradition is that of the exalted Christ with his Father (17:1,5,24).

This passage stresses the sinlessness of the life of the children of God. Many interpreters think these claims to be in conflict with the warning against supposing oneself to be sinless in 1:6,8 and the doctrine of forgiveness in 2:1f. They wonder how the author differs from his opponents.

Solutions to the dilemma frequently hypothesize a progressive understanding of perfection in 1 Jn—implied, it is claimed, by the eschatological reservation in v.2. This progressive doctrine is contrasted with the false reading of gnosticism as teaching that the gnostic cannot sin. We understand the author to be presenting a consistent picture of sin and perfection. The admonitions in chapter 1 derived from the baptismal tradition. The neophyte cannot enter the community without recognizing his or her need for the forgiveness made available in Christ. Chapter 2 distinguishes the possible sinfulness of the individual christian from the forgiveness which is always available. Here the author is primarily interested in the holiness and righteousness of the community in order to encourage his audience not to "go out from us." If the opponents were, as we have suggested, demanding a high degree of individual perfection, then the author must show that christians do possess the perfection they are accused of lacking. He is no more interested in the sins of a particular individual at this point than Paul was when he spoke of "walking according to the spirit" in Rom 8.

The community in which the spirit of God dwells can be said to possess perfection despite the transgressions of individuals. This combination emerges clearly among the essenes, who have elaborate legislation for members who mar the holiness and purity of the community, but who can also see the whole community as embodying the righteousness and perfection of God. What 1 Jn has refused to do is to adopt an option for holiness in which the community would follow a rigid code and exclude members who do not conform. He understands the forgiveness won by Jesus as making that approach unnecessary. At the same time, it is easy to see that the language about righteousness and purity derived from apocalyptic preaching could lead some christians to insist that individuals should embody that purity and perhaps even seek to dissociate themselves from those who did not do so. When we remember that the primary use of abiding language in the Johannine tradition is to enforce allegiance to the community when threatened, and that it does not refer to some private mystical experience, then it becomes clear that the author is insisting on the community as the place in which one finds perfection. He is not putting forth a philosophical doctrine of a soul purified from passions. (See Philo *de fug* cxxiv for such a psychological approach: the soul is incapable of sin as long as the divine word is within.)

Some interpreters claim that v.9 makes a community-based interpretation of the Johannine understanding of perfection impossible, because it expands the "born from God" language with the claim that those in whom God's seed dwells cannot sin. (RSV misleadingly translates "seed" as "nature" and has thus not only obscured the exegetical background of the passage but introduced a philosophical term which weights the interpretation of the passage in the direction of "sinless essence.") A brief look at some of the sources of the "seed" metaphor will explain its presence here. Within the epistle itself, you may notice that the previous verse refers back to the controversy with the jews in Jn 8. That controversy was introduced by their claim to be "seed of Abraham" and free. Jesus countered it by insisting that they do not do the righteousness characteristic of true sons of God since they reject his testimony and seek to kill him. We may suggest, then, that the "seed of God" image is another example of community language developed to distinguish christians from their jewish opposition. Philo (*vit. mos.* i, 279) speaks of the people of Israel as from a divine seed, which suggests that the christian title may have had jewish roots. Later the gnostics speak of themselves as "seed of Seth," the true sons of Adam as opposed to others derived from Cain or perhaps even to jews who also claimed descent from Seth. Both jewish and gnostic traditions have derived the "seed" metaphor from Genesis accounts of the true people of God. It is a group designation not an individual one. 1 Jn is about to appeal to Genesis explicitly when he introduces the Cain story in 3:12. The previous allusion to Jn 8 in combination with an explicit one to Genesis, to Cain as an example of "sin from the beginning," probably led to the introduction of the seed metaphor here. There is no reason to assume that 1 Jn has taken over the gnostic technical term being used by his opponents. We find other examples of Johannine self-designations, which we have already suggested were part of the community tradition, in verse 6 (know/see God).

The previous passage used apocalyptic images to castigate the author's opponents. Many expressions in this section have a similar ring. Apocalyptic preaching commonly divided humanity into two groups, the righteous and the wicked (sons of light and sons of darkness, or of Beliar). Sin is frequently defined as lawlessness (v.4; cf. Ps 32:1; Jer 31:34; Rom 4:7; Heb 10:17; 2 Thess 2:8 antichrist=man of lawlessness). It was also common to emphasize the deception that would characterize the last days. People would be led astray from righteousness into sin as in the traditional phrasing of v.7 (contrast the use of deceive in a doctrinal sense in 2:26).

Verse 8 allows the author to complete his identification of the two groups, using images derived from the fourth gospel. In the controversy with the jews in Jn 8, those who reject Jesus are called children of the devil, who show the passions of their father—especially, since they seek to kill Jesus—his being a murderer from the beginning (8:44). Here he is referred to as a "sinner from the beginning," but "murderer" is behind the more general "sinner." The author is about to introduce murder as the prime example of hating one's brother. Division of humanity into righteous, pure, over against sinners (vv.3,10) is common apocalyptic preaching. The author marks the transition between such traditional language and the central claim of the Johannine community when he makes "love for the brethren" the criterion for dividing the two groups (v.10b).

We see from this analysis of the author's language that he is not describing the spiritual state of individuals but the christian community as the true, righteous people of God. The claim in v.8 that Jesus appeared to "destroy the works of the devil" shows that he has the cosmic defeat of the power of evil in mind when he speaks of Jesus taking away sins (v.5) not simply particular sins of individuals. It is a fundamental conviction of Johannine theology that Jesus' coming accomplished the victory over evil which had been the object of so much apocalyptic preaching. He has established the community whose righteousness and holiness may be described in terms of God's dwelling with his people. We have seen 1 Jn refer to both God and Jesus with the expression "he is righteous" (2:29). Here traditional attributes of God, holiness and righteousness, refer both to the Father (vv.3 & 7) and to the Son, who is called "sinless" in v.5—though not in terms of his sacrificial death but as an indication of his essential identity with the Father. In chapters 1 & 2, the author alternated the light metaphor between God and Jesus; using it in both instances as paraenesis for how christians should "walk." He seems to be doing the same thing in this passage, since his primary focus is on the relationship between the christian and God. The christian is "begotten from Him." Thus we should not reduce the language of vv.3,5, & 7 to a doctrine of imitating virtues of Jesus. The author wishes to show that the community mirrors the perfection of its father. Perhaps he insists on the present reality of their status as children of God (v.2a) in response to the kind of christian apocalyptic preaching which deferred full adoption as sons to the future (e.g. Rom 8:14,19; Gal 3:26; 4:6f). The rest of this verse expresses the eschatological conviction that Jesus' full reality has yet to be seen. Although we cannot be certain of what the future of the believer will be like, we can be certain that it will be like the glorified state of Jesus (cf. Jn 17:24). Paul has a similar eschatological reservation when describing the resurrection of christians (Rom 8:29; 1 Cor 15:50f; 2 Cor 3:18). 1 Jn's reservation is not a way of saying that a person becomes progressively like Christ—a concept not introduced until christians began to assimilate the terminology of philosophical education. The reservation preserves the "in between" status of christian life without a heavy investment in an apocalyptic timetable about the impending end of the world. Though christians truly are children of God, their divine sonship is not the completion of the divine act of salvation. Verse 1 applies the contrast between their knowledge of the Father and the world's failure to acknowledge Jesus and hence those he sends (cp. Jn 15:18f,23; 16:3)—originally an answer to the puzzles of persecution—to the permanent life of the community (cf. Jn 17:15f). At the same time, the whole section implies that the opponents are to be associated with "the world" and "the children of the devil," and implies that their preaching is as much a threat and rejection of Jesus and the Father as was the earlier persecution.

LOVE THE BRETHREN.
3:11-18.

> [11]For this is the message which you have heard from the beginning, that we should love one another, [12]and not be like Cain who was of the evil one and murdered his brother. And why did he murder him? Because his own deeds were evil and his brother's righteous. [13]Do not wonder, brethren, that the world hates you. [14]We know that we have passed out of death into life, because we love the brethren. He who does not love remains in death. [15]Any one who hates his brother is a murderer, and you know that no murderer has eternal life abiding in him. [16]By this we know love, that he laid down his life for us; and we ought to lay down our lives for the brethren. [17]But if any one has the world's goods and sees his brother in need, yet closes his heart against him, how does God's love abide in him? [18]Little children, let us not love in word or speech but in deed and in truth.

1 Jn returns to the teaching on love which had been established in the traditional paraenesis of 2:7-11. He

continues the imagery from Jn 8 and the use of "world" as symbolic of all that is hostile to God's revelation as means of condemning the opponents. The story of Cain becomes an example of the most radical manner of hating a brother, murder. "Hatred of the brethren" does not refer to any particular ethical deviation of the author's opponents. The author is marshalling the resources of the community's tradition to reassure his audience. The opening formula is almost identical with 1:5. There the confession "God is light" introduced baptismal paraenesis. Here "love one another" is announced as *the message*; the teaching which the Johannine community saw as its very foundation (see above on 2:7-11).

Jude 11 refers to evil people as walking in the way of Cain. Abel is an example of righteousness and faith in Heb 11:4. A late gnostic work, *Valentinian Exposition*, preserves an old jewish tradition in which Cain and Abel represent the twofold division of humanity. Cain is inspired by the devil (the "murderer from the beginning" in Jn 8) when he murders his brother (CG XI *2* 38,24-33). Such a tradition may underlie Jn 8 and the author's selection of the Cain story here. The Johannine community may have used Cain as an example of the murderous intentions of the world during the persecution. They may even have spoken of the Jews as "seed of Cain" just as Jn 8 denies them the appellation "seed of Abraham." Hebrews shows that tradition associated righteousness with Abel as is the case here.

"Hatred by the world," which now appears frequently as an oblique reference to the opponents, is Johannine language from the earlier conflict (Jn 15:18f; 17:14). Verses 14-15 interpret the Cain story in terms of the love command. The expression "we have passed from death to life" comes from Jn 5:24. There it distinguishes those who believe in Jesus from those who do not; here, it distinguishes true christians from the opponents, who also claim to be christians.

The meaning of the love commandment is illustrated by the example of Jesus laying down his life (Jn 10:11,15, for his sheep; 15:13, for his "friends"). Though christians are encouraged to follow a similar example, it is clear that members of the Johannine community are no longer threatened with death for their faith. Verse 17 draws a more practical conclusion, which is typical early christian preaching (see Jas 2:14-17): one must be willing to share one's wealth with christians in need. The expression "world" in this verse refers to the transitory character of those material possessions for which people competed and in which they displayed such pride (see above on 2:16). Such preaching typically included the demand to express one's belief in deeds and not just words (v.18; cp. Jas 1:22; 2:15f; Mt 7:21).

OUR CONFIDENCE BEFORE GOD.
3:19-24.

> [19]By this we shall know that we are of the truth, and reassure our hearts before him [20]whenever our hearts condemn us; for God is greater than our hearts, and he knows everything. [21]Beloved, if our hearts do not condemn us, we have confidence before God; [22]and we receive from him whatever we ask, because we keep his commandments and do what pleases him. [23]And this is his commandment, that we should believe in the name of his Son Jesus Christ and love one another, just as he has commanded us. [24]All who keep his commandments abide in him, and he in them. And by this we know that he abides in us, by the Spirit which he has given us.

Confidence in their salvation was a key issue in the community (cp. 2:28f). This section of 1 Jn founds that confidence on the Johannine understanding of the true community of those who love each other as the abiding place of the spirit of God. For those who remain in that community, God guarantees salvation even against the accusations of one's own heart (vv.19-20). That claim is coherent with the fourth gospel's teaching that Jesus has already passed the judgment in his presence. The language of this section is so much less that of traditional early christian and Johannine preaching that it may well reflect the type of debate immediately affecting the community.

1 Jn 2:28-29 referred to the believer's confidence in the face of future judgment. Here the author goes further: even now the christian's heart should not condemn him (v.21). The fourth gospel uses the word translated "confidence" only in connection with the true community. In 16:25,29, Jesus now speaks "openly" with his disciples about the Father. The same gospel passage associates that speaking with the fact that the disciples can now approach the Father in prayer directly, since he loves those who believe in Jesus (Jn 16:26f; cf. 1 Jn 5:14; Jn 14:13f; 15:7; Mk 11:24 par). 1 Jn usually picks up language from the gospel that emphasizes the direct relationship between the christian and God as in the sayings on prayer in Jn 16 rather than that which implies some mediation by Jesus as in Jn 14. He wishes to found the christian's confidence on the new relationship with the Father. This relationship presupposes keeping his commandments (see also 1 Jn 2:3,4; 5:2f; 2 Jn 6; Jn 15:10, 15,21). The alternative expression "do what is pleasing to him" is typical paraenetic language (cf. Jn 8:29; Heb 13:21). Verse 23 summarizes "commandments" as belief in the name of His son and loving one another. We have seen the latter frequently as the epitome of Johannine paraenesis. This is the first time belief in Jesus appears. It will recur in future condemnations of the opponents (4:16; 5:1,20). The requirement of belief refers us back to similar demands in the fourth gospel where it is the guarantee of eternal life, of having passed through the judgment (Jn 5:24; 1 Jn 4:13; 5:5?). Thus, the author is still using the language of the gospel to make his case for the confidence he wishes to instill in his audience.

The concluding verses return to the theme of the indwelling of God with those who keep his commandments, but they also introduce a new motif in order to make the transition to the new section: God's indwelling is verified by the presence of the spirit in the community (3:24 = 4:13). The spirit's role is crucial to the Johannine understanding of the community as witness to the truth about Jesus as was already suggested in the discussion of anointing in 2:26f. It returns as guarantor of their teaching in the next section. Late jewish eschatology associated the presence of the spirit of God in the community with the new age. Its presence was felt to be anticipated in eschatological communities such as we find at Qumran (e.g. 1 QH 12.12; 13.19) and in early christianity (e.g. 1 Thess 4:8; Rom 5:5). The Johannine tradition seems to have moved beyond understanding the presence of the spirit as an indication of the elect community on the verge of the messianic age, to using images of the presence of the spirit, God or Jesus as guaranteeing its ongoing life and testimony to Jesus as the one sent by God.

One should not think from this passage in 1 Jn that members of the community were all afflicted by "guilt" in the modern psychological sense, or that they were suffering from the demands of an impossible ethic embodied in the love command as some interpreters have suggested. The crisis faced by the author has not been raised by the pastoral problem of dealing with individual "guilt feelings." It has been raised by those who questioned the Johannine understanding of salvation. The evidences which the author is suggesting to guarantee their certainty of salvation do not require the individual to feel some internal verification or manifestation of the spirit. They ask whether or not he or she belongs to the community in which the spirit of God dwells, to the community which is characterized by its belief in Jesus and its practice of brotherly love. That practice is not defined in psychological terms. An individual is not asked how he feels about his brother but whether he has helped a brother in need when he had the means to do so. This practical demand is rhetorically situated to come as something of a relief—following as it does the suggestion that one should be willing to die for a brother! Even if his heart should condemn him (and the author is not saying that it does), then God will guarantee his salvation.

TEST THE SPIRITS.
4:1-6.

> **4** Beloved, do not believe every spirit, but test the
> spirits to see whether they are of God; for many false
> prophets have gone out into the world. ²By this you know
> the Spirit of God: every spirit which confesses that Jesus
> Christ has come in the flesh is of God, ³and every spirit
> which does not confess Jesus is not of God. This is the
> spirit of antichrist, of which you heard that it was coming,
> and now it is in the world already. ⁴Little children, you
> are of God, and have overcome them; for he who is in you
> is greater than he who is in the world. ⁵They are of the
> world, therefore what they say is of the world, and the
> world listens to them. ⁶We are of God. Whoever knows
> God listens to us, and he who is not of God does not
> listen to us. By this we know the spirit of truth and the
> spirit of error.

The author returns to direct attack on his opponents by
once again invoking the ominous language of apocalyptic
preaching. Since he is still reading the present situation in
terms of past crises, we must continue to sift through his
rhetoric very carefully. The only certain indications 1 Jn
has given of the opponents' doctrine are that they have
denied the Johannine understanding of the death of Jesus
as atonement for the sins of christians and undermined
the community's confidence in their own salvation. In
response, he has taken great pains to show that the community of those who love one another has God present with
it in such a way as to establish both perfection and forgiveness. The message of chapter 4 largely reformulates these
earlier themes. Chapter 3 began by distinguishing two
groups of "children," those of God and those of the devil.
This chapter begins by distinguishing two spirits, truth and
error. A doctrine of "two spirits" was commonly associated
with two-ways paraenesis in which it accounts for good and
evil people. The author probably derived it from such

preaching. But he is not using it to make ethical distinctions in this passage; it accounts for the two types of christian teaching.

This section forms a neat rhetorical unity: the opening demand for distinguishing spirits concludes with the established separation of the two spirits at the end. That separation is accomplished by using the language of apocalyptic and Johannine dualism to present the audience with two clearly distinguished sides:

"us"	"them"
spirit of God (v.1)	spirit of antichrist (v.3)
spirit of God (v.1)	false prophets (v.1)
of God (v.4)	of the world (v.5)
confess Jesus Christ came in the flesh (v.2)	deny Jesus (v.3)
recognized by those who "know God" (v.6)	listened to by the world (v.5)
spirit of truth (v.6)	spirit of error (v.6)

With the exception of the confession in v.2, all the other assertions here have parallels either in apocalyptic preaching or in the Johannine reformulation of that language. The fourth gospel assured persecuted christians that although the religious authorities opposed them, they had the truth about Jesus. Their persecution is to be expected from a world which has rejected Jesus and his word (Jn 17:14). They possess the "spirit of truth" to guarantee their teaching (Jn 14:17,26; 16:13; and see the discussion of 1 Jn 2:20-22). Jn 17:25 contrasts Jesus who "knows the Father" and the disciples who "know that Jesus is sent from Him" with the world which does not know God. "Those who know God" (v.6) became one of the self-designations of Johannine christians (see above on 1 Jn 2:4). As in 1 Jn 2:18, apocalyptic predictions about antichrist and false prophecy are applied to the opponents. But rather than look toward future destruction of evil people, the Johannine tradition always emphasized the present victory of Jesus (and through him the christian) over evil or "the world." Now that he has cast the opponents in the negative role of "the world," the author may apply that victory language to his audience's relationship with them: God (or his spirit) is greater than the world (v.4; cp. Jn 17:14-16, Jesus asks the Father to protect his followers, who do not belong to the world, from the evil one).

The real exegetical problem in this section is the confession mentioned in v.2 and the associated testing of spirits. That confession reappears in 2 Jn 7 as a point about which the addressees might be deceived by false teachers. Notice that in v.3 the opponents are accused simply of denying Jesus. (The RSV has accepted a manuscript reading "do not confess" rather than the *luein*, lit. dissolve, destroy, preferred by most commentators. See Brown, *Community*: 111 n. 218. Brown's "negate the importance of" seems to us too interpretive a translation; Schnackenburg suggests "deny," while Bultmann has opted for a somewhat stronger "annul Jesus.") We have seen that it is a standard rhetorical tactic of the author to associate his opponents with those who in the earlier crisis really did deny the messiahship of Jesus or his being Son of God. This traditional confession is used in all the christological assertions in the epistles (1 Jn 2:22; 4:15; 5:1,5) except this passage and 2 Jn 7. We also know (e.g. Jn 17:25) that Jesus as "one sent from God" is a traditional christological slogan in Johannine circles. In order to be members of the community, 1 Jn's opponents must have accepted all these slogans even if the author does try to insinuate that they do not. Is the formulation in v.2 another traditional slogan from that earlier controversy? Or has the author taken a traditional confession "Jesus is the one sent from (coming from) God" and revised it to fit the new situation by adding "in the flesh"? In either case, one cannot reconstruct a christology of the opponents on the basis of this slogan.

Gnostic evidence does not support the kind of docetism frequently adduced for this passage. Although he realizes that problem (*Community*: 111-23), Brown still tries to use Johannine christological confessions to construct the christology of the opponents. It seems more likely that christology was not the real issue at all. 1 Jn has been concerned all along with problems of soteriology. The confidence of christians in salvation and forgiveness based on the atoning death of Jesus has been shaken (1:7; 2:2; 3:5; 4:10; 5:6; see Brown, *Community*: 121-23). The author may have updated an old slogan by adding "in flesh," but we cannot be sure whether his opponents would have been forced to reject that modification or not.

Commentators usually try to locate the "testing of spirits" within the context of early christian problems about testing, controlling, or legitimating prophetic or ecstatic phenomena within the life of the community. They rightly point out that our author shows no evidence of having to deal with the kind of ecstatic prophecy mentioned in 2 Thess 5:19f or 1 Cor 12:3-10, for example. Nor does he seem concerned with wandering preachers or wonder-workers who might preside over liturgical celebrations as in Did 11, either. We can perhaps gain some insight into what the author has in mind in v.2, if we begin with Houlden's suggestion (p. 108) that "confess" implies a liturgical context. Or, at least, a communal assembly of some sort. Oaths before the assembly played an important role in greek legal history. Development of courts and legal proceedings lessened the role played by such formal oaths, but one might still try to cut short a lengthly legal proceeding by demanding that one's opponent take an oath as to the facts of the case. Communities which relied solely on oral procedures for settling disputes and making agreements continued to place great weight on the formal oath taken before the assembly. It could even be that "christological slogans" played a role in the forensic proceedings to which christians had been subject during the persecution (see the way in which the Pharisees interrogate the blind man as to "who Jesus is" in Jn 9 for an example). The role that such slogans have in the language of the Johannine community suggests that initiation of new members may have been accompanied by pronouncing such confessions. Thus, we suggest that "testing the spirits" may be intended to have legal overtones: a person might be asked to "take an oath" in the presence of the community. The author may have devised the slogan in v.2 (and 2 Jn 7) as a model for use in such proceedings; as a way of testing those people whom he says are not really christians (2:19) and whose teaching should not be accepted.

There is no reason to assume from the expression "the world listens to them" (v.5) or "many" (2 Jn 7) that the opponents are successful and the Johannine position is failing to hold its ground (as Brown, *Community*: 142f). Apocalyptic rhetoric typically speaks of "many" being led astray. Verse 5 is just another of the author's appeals to the rhetoric of the fourth gospel to identify the opponents with the "unbelieving jews" (who are "from the world," Jn 8:23). As is the case with the issue of christology, one must be careful to identify the author's rhetoric before drawing factual conclusions.

LOVE IN THE CHRISTIAN COMMUNITY.
4:7-16a.

> [7]Beloved, let us love one another; for love is of God, and he who loves is born of God and knows God. [8]He who does not love does not know God; for God is love. [9]In this the love of God was made manifest among us, that God sent his only Son into the world, so that we might live through him. [10]In this is love, not that we loved God but that he loved us and sent his Son to be the expiation for our sins. [11]Beloved, if God so loved us, we also ought to love one another. [12]No man has ever seen God; if we love one another, God abides in us and his love is perfected in us.

> [13] By this we know that we abide in him and he in us, because he has given us of his own Spirit. [14] And we have seen and testify that the Father has sent his Son as the Savior of the world. [15] Whoever confesses that Jesus is the Son of God, God abides in him, and he in God. [16] So we know and believe the love God has for us.

We have chosen (with the Bible Society Greek New Testament) to divide verse 16, though the whole could belong to this section, and to take 16b "God is love" as the introduction to the next section (by analogy with 1:5). This whole part of 1 Jn is made up of short units which refer to tradition already known to the readers. It continues the author's policy of grounding the community and its tradition in its relationship to God himself. After expounding the principle "God is love" in vv. 7-10, the author applies it to the community in vv. 11-16a.

Verses 7-8 repeat a familiar point. Knowledge and perfection of divine love are tied to keeping the commandment, namely, loving one another (e.g. 2:4f). These verses make it clear that when the author speaks of love of God, he is thinking of God's love for humanity, and add the motif of being "born from God," which 2:29 applies to the person whose righteous behavior accords with the righteousness of God. The first section of 1 Jn made similar use of "God is light" to exhort christians to "walk in light." These examples point to an important feature of 1 Jn's use of divine attributes. They are not abstract statements about the nature of deity such as one might find in a philosophy of religion. Light, righteousness, love (and the "pure" and "sinless" applied to Jesus in 3:3,5, as well), are all derived from God's saving activity on behalf of humanity. The Johannine tradition sees that activity focused in Jesus, who is the light in which christians walk (1 Jn 2:8b); is righteous (3:7b), and is the revelation of the love of God (v.9; cp. Jn 3:16-18) and the source of their life (v.9; also 1:2; Jn 1:4; 3:16; 5:21b). Johannine tradition characteristically speaks of Jesus as "only begotten son" (cp. Jn

1:14-18; 3:16-18). In the fourth gospel, it served to emphasize the unique relationship between Jesus and God so as
to make him the only source of revelation about the Father.
Verse 10 expands verse 9, making it clear that the author
is not speaking about love of God as some human achievement. The "we ought to love one another" is not a way of
compelling a response from God, but itself derives from
the action God has taken on our behalf. 1 Jn thus expresses
a fundamental insight of the covenant theology of the
Old Testament as it had been handed on in christianity:
God takes the initiative in reconciling a sinful humanity
to himself (e.g. Rom 3:21-25; 8:32,39; see Schnackenburg:
233-35). Rom 3:21-25 ties that terminology with the sacrificial death of Jesus. 1 Jn, perhaps in opposition to his
opponents, also emphasizes the death of Jesus as reconciling sacrifice.

The move from the love of God shown in the death of
Jesus (v.10) to paraenesis (v.11) parallels the injunction
of 3:16. Verse 12 draws further consequences for christian
life from another favorite Johannine phrase about God, "no
one has seen him." In the fourth gospel, expressions like
"no one has seen God except the Son who makes him
known" (1:18; 3:13, only Jesus has ascended to heaven,
5:37, Jesus' opponents have never seen the Father, 6:46)
play an important role in the conflict with the jews. Contrary to jewish claims that Jesus is leading people astray,
Moses, Abraham and other prophets and visionaries whom
their tradition claims have seen God, have not done so.
Only Jesus has seen and can reveal the Father. Both Moses
(5:45) and Abraham (8:56) testify to him. This tradition
is the one to which the author now appeals. There is no
evidence that his opponents are claiming some mysticism
of individual ascent of the soul as commentators often
suppose. (Such piety is rarer among gnostics than many
interpreters would have us believe.) Rather, 1 Jn is appealing to a traditional slogan, used to establish Jesus as the
sole source of religious truth. He will draw an ethical
conclusion from that slogan just as he has been doing with

the statements about other divine attributes. God may be unseen by men, but his presence in the community is not. God abides with those who love one another. 1 Jn 2:5 made a parallel assertion: God's love for humanity is perfected in the one who keeps his word. There as here, that love is tied to confidence in abiding with God.

Verses 13-16 present other signs of the community's relationship with God. 1 Jn 4:13 repeats 3:24b—the phrase must have been a well-known formula. The introduction to v.14 recalls 1:1-4. It is followed by two traditional claims about Jesus. God has sent his son, a persistent theme in the gospel (e.g. 3:17, above v.10), and Jesus is savior of the world (Jn 4:46, where it shows the universality of Jesus' mission). "Jesus is Son of God" was also an important confessional formula in the community (cf. 1 Jn 5:5). Verse 15b expands the Son of God title with the abiding language so typical of the Johannine way of referring to the presence of God in the community. This expansion is not a new development in the tradition. Jn 14:10 explains that the works Jesus has done are from the Father abiding in him. Therefore, we assume that vv.14-15 are repeating the community's traditional understanding of the relationship between Jesus and the Father, which is the basis for his revelation of the Father's love. Verse 16a forms an *inclusio* with v.11: the community is convinced of God's love.

GOD'S LOVE AS OUR CONFIDENCE.
4:16b-21.

> God is love, and he who abides in love abides in God, and God abides in him. [17]In this is love perfected with us, that we may have confidence for the day of judgment, because as he is so are we in this world. [18]There is no fear in love, but perfect love casts out fear. For fear has to do with punishment, and he who fears is not perfected in love. [19]We love, because he first loved us. [20]If any one

says, "I love God," and hates his brother, he is a liar; for he who does not love his brother whom he has seen, cannot love God whom he has not seen. [21]And this commandment we have from him, that he who loves God should love his brother also.

The second "God is love" (16b; cf. 8b) returns to the theme of christian confidence. It provides the most radical grounding of that confidence yet—though one not materially different from the previous two. 1 Jn 2:28 grounded confidence in the judgment in the justice of God toward those who also do righteousness. The most traditional of the three passages, it could well derive from jewish teaching. In 3:21-24, confidence in prayer is founded on the direct relationship to the Father enjoyed by those who believe in Jesus, keep his command of love, and to whom the Father has given his spirit. Here, God's action in showing his love is the basis for confidence and for the love christians are to show one another. Verse 16b repeats the themes of 3:24 and 4:13,15. Everything 1 Jn has been saying about Jesus' advocacy and the resulting freedom from sin is summarized in the vision of God's love for humanity reaching its goal in this community of love. Verse 17 applies the indwelling language to the life of the believer. "Just as he is so are we in this world" must refer to the author's application of divine attributes to the believer's life as the basis for both his confidence and his behavior.

Though some commentators suppose that the opponents had a piety of direct vision of God that was undermining the teaching about love for fellow christians, the evidence is too weak to support such a connection. It is more likely that the distinction between "saying one loves God" and actually loving fellow christians is the Johannine formulation of the common paraenetic distinction between merely saying and actually doing (cp. 1 Jn 3:18). Some scholars suggest that v.21 is the Johannine formulation of the double command of love of God and neighbor (Mk 12:28-34 par) rather than a variant of the single command "love one another" from Jn 13:34. Such a form of the double command might have been part of the synoptic-like Jesus tradition that circulated in the Johannine community. The double form of the injunction appears when the theme of mutual love reappears in 5:2. There it is combined with the earlier formulation about keeping God's commandments.

THE VICTORY OF OUR FAITH.
5:1-5.

> **5** Every one who believes that Jesus is the Christ is a child of God, and every one who loves the parent loves the child. [2]By this we know that we love the children of God, when we love God and obey his commandments. [3]For this is the love of God, that we keep his commandments. And his commandments are not burdensome. [4]For whatever is born of God overcomes the world; and this is the victory that overcomes the world, our faith. [5]Who is it that overcomes the world but he who believes that Jesus is the Son of God?

This section makes the transition between the previous discussion of mutual love and the concluding return to the theme of testimony, which will form an inclusio with the opening of 1 Jn. It is sometimes taken as part of the previous discussion. However, two traditional expressions of Johannine belief frame the section as an independent unit. Verses 1-3 reformulate the previous statements about loving God and keeping his commandment of love. The author has used a variety of formulations to connect "being born from God" and keeping the commandments: he is righteous (2:29); does not sin (3:9, seed of God); loves (4:7). 1 Jn 5:1b is the positive expression of the negative one in 4:20a: "Everyone who loves the one who begets (RSV "the father") loves the one begotten (RSV "child")." The author may be quoting an aphorism or proverb well-known in the community. Compared with 4:20b the continuation in v.2 seems a bit paradoxical, although the author must still be reformulating the previous passage. How can "love for God" be the sign of love for "the children of God"? Rather than emend the text as some scholars do, we would concur with the suggestion of others that the author means us to understand "love God and keep his commandments" as a single expression (cp. 2:3, knowledge of God is keeping his commands; 3:10b, children of God do righteousness; 4:21, love of God and brother). Verse 3 reinforces this interpretation. The variation in v.2, then, is closest to the specification of love in terms of behavior toward the christian in need that 3:17 presented as the practical interpretation of "laying down one's life for the brethren." There is nothing esoteric about love for God or for one's fellow christian in 1 Jn. It is demonstrated in the behavior of christians toward each other. Verse 3b adds the claim that these commands are not burdensome. Some interpreters see this verse—like 4:21—as another allusion to the Johannine tradition of the sayings of Jesus (cp. Mt 11:30). Others see it as derived from the jewish insistence that the Law is not burdensome (cf. Deut 30:11). Whatever its source, this saying could well have been an important part of the community's teaching when it had to define its own interpretation of the commands of God against the hostile claims of jewish teachers.

Verses 4-5 return to another theme of Johannine preaching, the christian's victory over sin or the evil one. 1 Jn 2:12-14 tied together forgiveness of sins; knowing the Father and Jesus and victory over the evil one. "World" here is equivalent to the evil one. It carries the same negative sense that it did in the exhortation not to love the world which followed the previous victory proclamation (2:15). This victory is part of the reality of the believer's life because Jesus as Son of God has already overcome the evil one/ world (Jn 12:31; 16:33). He does not have to reappear as judge and divine warrior to destroy Satan and evil people in order to win the victory that God had been promising his people. Some interpreters associated v.5 with the use of the victory theme against the opponents in 4:4. If the victory is one against false teaching, as that association might suggest, then this verse might be the lead into the next section on testimony. 1 Jn 5:6 also looks toward what is the traditional testimony by revising it to combat the opponents, and is thus related to 5:5. We have chosen to see 5:5 as an inclusio with 5:1 on the basis of its use of a traditional christological confession.

GOD'S TESTIMONY TO HIS SON.
5:6-13.

> [6]This is he who came by water and blood, Jesus Christ, not with the water only but with the water and the blood. [7]And the Spirit is the witness, because the Spirit is the truth. [8]There are three witnesses, the Spirit, the water, and the blood; and these three agree. [9]If we receive the testimony of men, the testimony of God is greater; for this is the testimony of God that he has borne witness to his Son. [10]He who believes in the Son of God has the testimony in himself. He who does not believe God has made him a liar, because he has not believed in the testimony that God has borne to his Son. [11]And this is the testimony, that God gave us eternal life, and this life is in his Son. [12]He who has the Son has life; he who has not the Son of God has not life.
>
> [13]I write this to you who believe in the name of the Son of God, that you may know that you have eternal life.

This section is dominated by the word "testimony," which appeared in the opening (1:2); was alluded to at 4:14, but has not yet been expanded. Testimony played an important role in the fourth gospel which expressed the encounter between Jesus and the world in forensic metaphors. The world is judged by its response to Jesus and his victory over its ruler. The most important sources for the language of this section are the controversy stories in Jn 5 and 8. (The reference to testimony by the spirit of truth in v.7 may also hark back to Jn 15:26.)

Verse 6 goes beyond the confession of Jesus as Son of God to deal with his death as atonement. This theme is linked with baptismal symbolism. If you turn back to the story of Jesus' baptism in the gospel of John (Jn 1:29-34), you will see that 1 Jn assumes his readers know that version of the story. The gospel narrative has reinterpreted the traditional story so that it is not a baptism at all but John the Baptist's proclamation of Jesus as lamb who takes away the sin of the world (see Perkins: 12-14). That proclamation is part of the testimony the Baptist gives throughout the first chapter and follows what he has just told the jews about his own mission (Jn 1:19-28). You will also notice that the coming of the spirit does not apply as much to Jesus—as in the synoptic versions—as to the Baptist. The latter's vision of the spirit is God's revelation to him that Jesus is his Son. Verse 6 alludes to the baptismal story in such a way as to insist that God's (= the spirit's) testimony to Jesus is not just associated with baptism (and Jesus' bringing the spirit) but with his death.

Verses 7-8 are designed to emphasize the testimony to Jesus' death: it is impossible to separate the testimony of the spirit from water and blood. This verse also reminds the audience of an interpretation of the passion story common in Johannine circles and reflected in Jn 19:34b-35, water and blood flow from the side of the crucified Jesus. Scholars also suggest that the author may be referring beyond the gospel stories of the baptism and death of Jesus to the sacramental life of the community. The fourth gospel shows baptism—spirit (3:5) and participation in the eucharistic celebration of the death of Jesus (6:53) as necessary for a person to receive the eternal life brought by Jesus. Jn 19:35 referred to human testimony about the death of Jesus. In Jn 5:33,36, Jesus refers his opponents to the testimony they had received from the Baptist as human testimony. He says that he has no need of such human testimony, since he has the greater testimony of the Father (5:37f; 8:18) both in the works the Father has given him, i.e. to judge and give life (5:36; 10:25), and in the Father's word, scripture (5:39). The reference to the Baptist's testimony probably led 1 Jn to combine allusion to that story with the language of Jn 5. He insists that although the community does have human testimony, the real witness to Jesus is the Father himself, as he has become known to them through the Son. Verse 10 invokes Jn 8:18, the Father's testimony to Jesus. The failure of Jesus' audience to receive his word (or the Father's testimony) shows their father to be a liar, the devil; were Jesus to accept their views he would be a liar as well (8:44,55). 1 Jn comments that people who will not receive God's testimony to his own Son in fact make God a liar. (A positive formulation of v. 10 appears in Jn 3:33, the person who receives Jesus' testimony about the Father is said to "set his seal on the fact that God is true.")

Verses 11 and 12 give the testimony about the Son as it applies to the christian: God has given eternal life to the one who believes in the Son (cp. Jn 3:15f,36; 17:2f; and especially 5:24,26 discussed in connection with 1 Jn 3:14). In other words, the author is not referring to some new, inner experience of certainty but to the existence of a community of believers who are confident that God's love has been shown in his having given them eternal life through Jesus. That community itself is testimony to the truth of the faith as the author has presented it. Verse 12 repeats the demand that a person believe in order to have life (cp. 1 Jn 2:23; 2 Jn 9).

The conclusion, v. 13, echoes the conclusion of the gospel (20:31). Since the audience is christian, the author reformulates his conclusion slightly so as to insist that they know that they have eternal life. Once again, we are faced with the real crisis behind 1 Jn: peoples' faith in their salvation has been shaken, but not their faith in Jesus as Son of God.

APPENDIX: THE COMMUNITY DEALS WITH SIN. 5:14-21.

> [14]And this is the confidence which we have in him, that if we ask anything according to his will he hears us. [15]And if we know that he hears us in whatever we ask, we know that we have obtained the requests made of him. [16]If any one sees his brother committing what is not a mortal sin, he will ask, and God will give him life for those whose sin is not mortal. There is sin which is mortal; I do not say that one is to pray for that. [17]All wrongdoing is sin, but there is sin which is not mortal.
>
> [18]We know that any one born of God does not sin, but He who was born of God keeps him, and the evil one does not touch him.
>
> [19]We know that we are of God, and the whole world is in the power of the evil one.
>
> [20]And we know that the Son of God has come and has given us understanding, to know him who is true; and we are in him who is true, in his Son Jesus Christ. This is the true God and eternal life. [21]Little children, keep yourselves from idols.

Verse 13 might have seemed a fitting conclusion, but the author has one further set of instructions and one more way of drawing the distinctions between the community and "the world." Perhaps the allusion to confidence in eternal life in v. 13 touched off this final instruction. Like the rest of the work, it is largely traditional material. The section falls into two parts: the community's confident prayer to the Father (vv. 14-17) and the separation of those who serve God from a world under the dominion of Satan (vv. 18-21).

The section is the most direct reflection of community rules that we find in the Johannine writings even though much of the early language of 1 Jn had parallels in essene rules and in Didache. The author begins with the theme of confidence in prayer that is according to the will of God (cp. 1 Jn 3:21f). But he is not dealing with petitionary or intercessory prayer in general. He is referring to formal acts of prayer in the community. Mt 18:15-20 illuminates this passage. It describes legal proceedings to be taken in christian communities to win back a brother who has sinned. There are three elements in the process. First, there are steps to be taken in admonishing and bringing back the brother: private conversation, private conversation with witnesses, and if that fails, public presentation before the community. (The essenes also had detailed procedures for bringing a grievance against a fellow member before the leaders of the community.) You will have noticed, of course, that Matthew places this legislation within the context of Jesus' teaching on forgiveness by having him tell Peter that there is no limit to the number of times an erring brother can be forgiven. Second, someone who refuses to acknowledge the decision of the community assembly is excluded. Members are no longer to associate with him—he becomes as a "tax-collector and sinner." Third, the authority to make such judgments is grounded in two sayings of Jesus: His gift of the power of binding and loosing and his presence at the prayer of the gathered community (2 or 3 were the required number of witnesses). *James* also mentions such community assemblies. Jas 2:1-7 warns against partiality towards the rich in rendering judgment. (Jewish law also contained rules against allowing the social status of litigants be indicated either in their dress or in the way in which they were seated.) Jas 5:16-20 mentions community prayer for the sick, for forgiveness of sinners, and finally the efforts—including prayer—which brothers should make to return a sinner to the community. Thus the connection between confident prayer and winning back the erring member is securely established in early christian community rules. These rules form the context out of which this passage is speaking. The erring brothers in this particular case would be the opponents.

But Matthew shows that there were also limits to what a community could tolerate. Forgiveness can be extended any number of times, but a person who refuses to acknowledge the judgment of the assembly cannot continue to be a member. In 1 Cor 5 Paul demanded exclusion of a notorious sinner. The essenes too had various degrees of exclusion from association with members of the community. A person might be excluded from association with the general membership to be rebuked by the teachers of the community until he repented. But someone who had been in the community over 10 years and lapsed could never return. All members of the sect are to avoid such a person, and are exhorted in general not to enter into relationships or even religious discussions with "those of ill repute" (e.g. 1 QS 7.18-25).

These rules and warnings help us understand the "sin unto death" (RSV "mortal sin") and the language of separation in vv.18-21. Originally, the "sin unto death" was probably the reverse of the belief in Jesus that brings eternal life, that is, denying one's belief in Jesus during persecution. We have already seen what a crucial role slogans about Jesus had come to play in the identity and language of Johannine christians. Those who deny Jesus are excluded from life (1 Jn 2:22f). Oaths of allegiance may have been required during those times. 1 Jn 4:2 suggests an attempt to impose such an oath on the opponents. Note that the language of "listen/not listen" appears in the context of the judicial assembly in Mt 18.

Verses 18-20 use images from Jn 17 to reinforce the separation of christians from outsiders. These metaphors had been an important source of self-identity during the time of persecution. 2 Jn 10-11 show that the author would like to apply a rule of non-association to the opponents such as we find in the various community rules. The warning against idolatry (v.21) may be associated with such rules. In the Old Testament idolatry indicated apostasy from judaism; for the essenes, departure from the teaching of the sect though not necessarily from judaism. In 1 Jn the opponents are christians, not outsiders who would lead a person to deny Jesus altogether. The author has their false teaching in mind when he warns his audience to avoid idols. The opponents fit the characteristics of those the essenes will not allow to return to the sect if they lapse. They have been members for a long time but have left ("gone out from us," 2:19). They seem to be engaged in encouraging other christians in the Johannine community to follow their lead. When 1 Jn says that there is no prayer for such people (a reapplication of an earlier rule about apostates during persecution?), he suggests both that they cannot be reconciled with the community and that members should not associate with them even for the purpose of trying to bring them back as they would do for any brother who was in sin. We learn in 2 Jn that they also fit the criterion of Mt 18 in not acknowledging the authority of the elder, the "listen to us" of 4:5. Thus, once again the author identifies his opponents as christians no longer but as those who belong to the world, who are opposed to God.

Some people have found this position extremely harsh for someone who stresses the centrality of mutual love in the identity of the christian community and in its vision of God. First of all, it is clear that love is never indiscriminate acceptance of a person no matter what. It is defined by specific ways of treating fellow christians, which cross social barriers, like sharing one's goods with the needy. Secondly, although the author's rhetoric implies that the opponents "hate the brethren," he has no specific moral charge against them. But the effect their preaching is having in the community is another matter. He wishes to show that rejecting Jesus' death as atonement for sin strikes at a central manifestation of divine love for humanity. Later gnostics are quite capable of conceiving the love of God in his sending Jesus to redeem those imprisoned in sin and darkness; they might even have argued that the best one can make of the death of the revealer is that it shows up the inherent hostility to the divine which is characteristic of this world, but to suppose that a loving God would tolerate or worse demand the death of his Son is ludicrous. The crisis in the Johannine community seems to have fallen on the pastoral side. Baptism, forgiveness through Jesus' intercession, and atoning death were all ways in which the community saw itself called to a degree of sinlessness and perfection that could give testimony to Jesus and divine love in a hostile world. Their crisis of confidence might even undermine another central insight of the Johannine tradition: Jesus has won the victory over sin and death so that forgiveness, eternal life and friendship with God belong to christians now. They are not contingent on a future judgment. The author has tried to use the Johannine tradition of ethical teaching, its insights about God and confession of Jesus to motivate mutual love and confidence without appeal to burdensome legal rules or strict ascetic purification. Because the author sees that the opponents' position threatens fundamental truths of Johannine christianity, he adopts a rather rigid position toward those responsible for the preaching.

His characterization of the separateness of the community in vv. 18-20 collects metaphors by which Johannine christians had traditionally expressed their unique status over against external hostility. They alone have salvation and life from the true God (v. 20). These verses can be best understood as a sustained allusion to Jn 17. Christ keeps christians from sin; from the power of the evil one (v. 18; Jn 17:12,15; 1 Jn 3:6). They are not of the world, which is in the power of the evil one (v. 19; Jn 17:16; 1 Jn 4:4-6). Jesus' coming has given them true understanding of the Father (v. 20; Jn 17:6-8,14,17; 1 Jn 2:12-14,20f). The result of their knowledge is unity with the Father and Jesus (Jn 17:21, 23,26; 1 Jn 3:24; 4:13) and eternal life (17:2f; 1 Jn 1:2; 2:25). Some commentators also suggest that Jesus' refusal to pray for the world (Jn 17:9) is the basis for the refusal to pray for those who have committed the "sin unto death" (v. 16c)— a rule that may have come into being during the persecution when christians denied their belief in Jesus rather than be excluded from the synagogue. 1 Jn invokes that rule against the opponents just as he has applied all the other negative imagery from that conflict to them.

Because Johannine language is always in terms of I (Jesus); we or you (pl) and them, and says nothing explicit about the internal organization of christian communities, people tend to interpret its piety as centered on the individual and his or her faith, on experience of the indwelling of Father or Son, and on the individual's love of God or personal sins. 1 Jn has no indication of any such personal piety. On the contrary, the author presupposes community discernment of the true tradition. The language of his paraenesis is directed toward the community of believers, not toward individual experiences of faith. His use of the language of the fourth gospel as community instruction and self-identification probably indicates the way that language was generally understood. Persecution seems to have intensified the images of mutual love and solidarity in opposition to a hostile world. Perhaps it even left Johannine christianity disinclined to develop community structures along the authoritarian lines of the synagogue, since religious leaders and teachers had been the source of persecution. No individual authorities guarantee the tradition. The author appeals to the testimony of the community as a whole as would be the case in circles still influenced by oral modes of learning and perception. Tradition is in the common memory and testimony. The author's style of allusion, use of short formulae, repetition and variation all suggest oral modes of learning. The traditions of the community were not labored over as texts but spoken aloud and held in memory either as stories of Jesus or as general rules, aphorisms, or short formulae which identified belief in Jesus, community identity, or proper christian conduct. In such communities, there is no concept of the faith experience of private individuals apart from their belonging to the community. You can see that exclusion from that community is also a much more serious matter for them! One must belong to the community of those who "know God," "love the brethren" etc. The author of 1 Jn does not give us enough information to tell whether his opponents really preached an individual piety and asceticism as is often suggested. What we can see is his mobilizing all the authority of the community's tradition and past experience, of its language and story, of its paraenesis and rite, to focus an identity, an image of God and salvation, that will confirm the confidence of his audience in the salvation and victory that is theirs as long as they remain in that community of believers.

Two and Three John

LETTERS FROM THE ELDER

The Letter Form

TWO AND THREE JOHN have the length and format of the type of private letters that survive in abundance from the graeco-roman period. Letters have four sections:

(1) *Opening*: "from x to y, greetings"

(2) *Health wish*: the opening is often, though not always, followed by wishes for the good health of the addressee; sometimes a report about the sender's health, or an indication of those from whom the sender has had news of the addressee. Sometimes a health wish appears at the end of a letter instead.

(3) *Body*: The writer states whatever business has prompted the letter. The body may conclude with reference to the sender's travel plans, if these have not been the main subject of the letter; or with a recommendation for the person bringing the letter, if the letter as a whole is not one of recommendation. Both occur at the end of 3 Jn.

(4) *Closing*: "farewell." Sometimes the closing includes greetings to other members of the family to which the sender writes or to friends or from people who are with him. Private letters are typically short. They contain only as much information as is necessary to convey the sender's message.

With the exception of Philemon, the Pauline letters are obviously something of an anomaly. They are much longer and devote themselves to instructing the community. But

73

some of the innovations of the Pauline letter also appear in 2-3 Jn. The greeting and closing are expanded with benedictions. The health wish is usually replaced by an expression of gratitude for the fidelity to christian faith of the community to which the author is writing. Naturally, since he was a travelling missionary, Paul usually has references to plans to visit the communities in question. 2-3 Jn show shorter elaborations in these directions but remain within the length and format of a private letter. Some commentators make a great deal over differences in language and style between 2-3 Jn and 1 Jn or the fourth gospel. However, these differences are not so great that they could not be accounted for by noting that the latter are intended as formal statements of the tradition, they use its public language, and were probably read aloud. 2-3 Jn, on the other hand, represent private style rather than public exposition.

Author, Addressees, Context

Interpreters disagree about the extent to which 1-3 Jn may be used to interpret each other. Some treat them all as phases in the history of a single, worsening conflict. (Diotrephes turns the table on the elder in 3 Jn.) They see progress from general admonition against false teachers (1 Jn), to having them expelled (2 Jn), to being expelled by them (3 Jn). As will become evident in the exegesis, we do not favor such a construction. 1-2 Jn seem to be concerned with the same problem. On our reading of 1 Jn 5:14-21, the elder's position against associating with false teachers is the same in both. 3 Jn deals with a different problem.

One of the difficulties in assessing these letters is the lack of specific details about the sender in 2-3 Jn and the addressee in 2 Jn. The author simply refers to himself as "the elder." In the pastoral epistles, that term is the title of a specific office within the community (cf. 1 Tim 5:15), but there is no indication of such an office in Johannine circles. The author never appeals either to apostolic authority or to authority that he holds from the community—unlike the pastoral epistles. Therefore, most scholars assume that "elder" was an honorary title given a well-known christian by communities who honored his teaching but were not formally bound to his authority. This informal authority may be reflected in a letter from 4th century Egypt. A member of a small christian sect writes to ask for aid for a christian who has gone bankrupt and whose children have been taken by creditors. (*Selected Papyri* I #160, Loeb Classical Library; this is the concrete side of the love command!) The addressee is obviously a person of some wealth and influence in the community, since the sender expects that he will be able to help this unfortunate christian out of his difficulties. The name of the addressee on the outside is followed by "elder." We suggest that no ecclesiastical office is involved in this case either. Rather, "elder" indicates a person of wealth and standing within the larger community. Such usage fits the context of 2-3 Jn and authority in Johannine communities very well.

A second puzzle in the opening of 2 Jn lies in the failure to specify the addressee. Some scholars have supposed that the expression "elect lady" refers to an individual rather than to a community. "Lady" (or the masculine "lord") frequently appears in the opening of letters from children to parents—or, more generally, where the sender is in a relationship of dependence on the addressee, as in the unusual case when a father addresses his son in that fashion. They propose that "lady" refers to a woman of wealth and influence, probably the person in whose house the local church met. Both the Pauline letters and Acts give examples of christian communities meeting in the homes of such women (e.g. Philm 2; 1 Cor 1:11; Col 4:15; Acts 12:12; 16:14). The church in a given area seems to have been made up of a number of such smaller groups which gathered in individuals' homes. However, this interpretation founders on the author's use of "children of your elect sister" to refer to christians with him who also send greetings to the community addressed. Another suggestion is that the lack of specific addressee—or at least a region to which the letter is going—shows that 2 Jn is not a letter at all. Rather, they suggest that it was composed on the basis of 1 Jn to be used by travelling missionaries to impose sanctions against false teachers by appealing to the authority of the author of 1 Jn. Copies of 1 Jn may have been circulated with it. We think that 1 Jn itself intends sanctions against false teachers, and, finding no difference in outlook between the two letters, suppose that the author of 1 Jn composed 2 Jn, perhaps as a cover letter for 1 Jn, and directed it to communities besides his own threatened by the preaching of the false teachers.

3 Jn, on the other hand, seems to be concerned with a different problem. Christians who travelled from place to place depended on local communities, house churches, for hospitality and assistance. Not surprisingly, hospitality is frequently mentioned as a key christian virtue (cf. Heb 13:1f, the first example of brotherly love is hospitality; Rom 16:1f; 1 Pet 4:9). These travellers also carried letters and news from one community to another. In 3 Jn, the elder needs to obtain hospitality for his associates after they have been denied it by another group under the influence of a man called Diotrephes. Presumably the two groups are house churches in the same area.

It has almost become customary to assume that Diotrephes was assuming the leadership role of a monarchic bishop known to us from the letters of Ignatius of Antioch, and that the "elder," representing the older charismatic style of leadership, stands opposed to this development of ecclesiastical office (Von Campenhausen: 141; Schnackenburg: 301). Just as there is no evidence that Diotrephes was associated with the false teachers, there is also no evidence for such a conflict over church order. The Johannine language tradition lacked the type of symbolism to which hierarchical ordering of the community could attach itself. That gap may have inhibited the development of community structures. We also know that the people who formed the trade associations and private clubs for the worship of a favorite deity, often sought to replicate in miniature the kind of hierarchy, honor and status that they saw imposed on them from above by the rich and powerful. There are plenty of references in the New Testament to indicate that such tendencies caused problems in early christian communities, which emphasized the equality of members and refused to let an individual's wealth or social status entitle him or her to special privilege. The simplest reading of 3 Jn is to assume that Diotrephes is an ambitious person, perhaps of some wealth in the community, perhaps even the head of a house church. He wants to enjoy the same kind of influence and authority in his church that the elder enjoys both in his own and in others in which he does not live. Such ambition may not represent the ideal of christian fellowship, but it would hardly be unusual within the context of roman social relations.

We conclude, then, that 2-3 Jn give us glimpses into the private relationships of Johannine christians. They also show us that the Johannine community was not just a single group but was spread over a region—that around the city of Ephesus? (so Brown, *Community*: 99). The Johannine writings indicate several different groups: that in which the elder lives; the group or groups to which 2 Jn is addressed; that around Diotrephes, and another (in the same region?) around Gaius. These communities are linked by the travelling of missionaries and others from one to the other and by their common Johannine tradition.

TWO JOHN

AVOID FALSE TEACHERS

Outline

2 JN CAN BE outlined easily following the model of the private letter presented in the previous section:

(1) *Opening*: vv.1-3. Note that the standard short greeting has been expanded with a benediction in v.3.

(2) *Health wish*: Missing. But we find a version of its Pauline equivalent, the thanksgiving for the faith of the addressees in v.4. (Paul usually speaks of giving thanks to God; the elder speaks only of his own satisfaction with the community.)

(3) *Body*: vv.4-11. The author presents the real business of the letter: no dealings with false teachers. Note that he presents his suggestion as a petition (v.5); not as an authoritative command.

(4) *Closing*: vv.12-13. It includes potential travel plans and the greeting from members of the author's community. We have already observed the peculiarity of this letter over against the usual private letter, its lack of detailed address. Perhaps it was intended for more than one group that made up the Johannine church in the area.

GREETING.
1-3.

> The elder to the elect lady and her children, whom I love in the truth, and not only I but also all who know the truth, ²because of the truth which abides in us and will be with us forever:

> [3]Grace, mercy, and peace will be with us, from God the Father and from Jesus Christ the Father's Son, in truth and love.

"Elder" is an honorary title, not an ecclesiastical office. It indicates that the person was someone of position and respect within the community. "Elect," a jewish term for the faithful people of God, is often used of christians (e.g. 1 Pet 5:13). Paul often refers to members of his churches as "children" (e.g. 1 Cor 4:14; 2 Cor 6:13; Gal 4:19). "Children" was also a favorite self-designation among Johannine christians. "Beloved" is another common form of address (1 Jn 4:1; cf. 2 Tim 1:2). The author adds "in truth" to his expression of love for the community. Though the phrase could be merely adverbial, "truly," the author uses "truth" as a catchword for the opening section. He uses "truth" in its full theological import, revelation of the Father in Jesus (Jn 1:8; 2:4 etc.) Johannine christians also apparently referred to themselves as "those who know the Father/God" (see above 1 Jn 2:4). "Those who know the truth" as descriptive of christians in v.1b is a variant of that tradition. Verse 2 makes the same point by using another favorite metaphor "abiding in/with" (cf. Jn 14:16f, with spirit of truth). Once again the author is expressing the Johannine understanding of community as the place in which divine presence is found. The author may have centered the opening around "truth" because he intends to oppose the false teachers.

The benediction of v.3 is typical of christian modifications of the jewish "grace and peace" (as in Gal 6:16; Jud 2) to a three-part "grace, mercy and peace" (e.g. 1 Tim 1:2; 2 Tim 1:2, note that Timothy is "my true child in the faith"; such language about "truth and faith" characterizes later christian writings faced with the problem of diverse christian teaching). Pauline examples show what was probably the usual ending, "from God the Father and Jesus Christ our Lord." 2 Jn 3 in typically Johannine fashion has "Jesus

Christ the Father's Son." The final "in truth and love" is an inclusio and leads into the next section—a simpler example of a mode of composition common in 1 Jn. The body of the letter will follow a typically Johannine progression. The author will appeal to the community's tradition of love for one another as command from God before turning to attack the false teaching of the opponents and suggesting measures to be taken against them.

WALK IN LOVE.
4-6.

> [4]I rejoiced greatly to find some of your children following the truth, just as we have been commanded by the Father. [5]And now I beg you, lady, not as though I were writing you a new commandment, but the one we have had from the beginning, that we love one another. [6]And this is love, that we follow his commandments; this is the commandment, as you have heard from the beginning, that you follow love.

We have seen that the *captatio benevolentiae* of v.4 substitutes for the usual health wish after the greeting. It also provided the transition to the body of the letter. As in the opening paraenesis of 1 Jn, "walk in truth" refers to living according to the teaching of the community. It is not clear whether "I have found" refers to an actual visit the elder made to the area, to a visit made to his community by christians from that area, or is simply a literary formalism by which the author can associate himself with those whose faithfulness he praises. Some interpreters think that the expression "some of your children" indicates that the author knows that false teachers have already gained a hearing in the community to which he is writing. We saw in 1 Jn that he habitually insinuates that his opponents "do not love the brethren" even though there is no evidence that their position implied immorality.

The opening of v.5 suggests that the letter is a petition; not a command. Petitionary letters frequently begin by stating the background of the case or of the sender's (or his family's) relationship to the addressee before they get around to the actual request. So here. A condensed summary of the community's paraenesis and characterization of the opponents as "apocalyptic enemies" precedes the actual request in v.10. This two-part thrust is typical of the composition in 1 Jn: first the author states the paraenetic tradition, which sets the identity of the community; then he makes a direct attack on the opponents using the rhetoric of apocalyptic preaching.

Verse 5 introduces what 1 Jn has shown us is the command in Johannine ethical preaching: love one another (1 Jn 3:11,27; 4:7,11f). Also, typically, this teaching is presented as known "from the beginning," i.e. such teaching has been given the audience since they first became christians (1 Jn 2:7-9, the expression also has overtones of being part of the truth revealed in Jesus as in 1 Jn 1:1). 2 Jn 6 reads like a reformulation of 1 Jn 2:3-7. We find the combination of love of God, keeping His commandments, and exhortation about how one is to "walk" which is expressed in more elaborate form in 1 Jn 2:3-7.

BEWARE OF THE DECEIVERS.
7-9.

> [7]For many deceivers have gone out into the world, men who will not acknowledge the coming of Jesus Christ in the flesh; such a one is the deceiver and the antichrist. [8]Look to yourselves, that you may not lose what you have worked for, but may win a full reward. [9]And one who goes ahead and does not abide in the doctrine of Christ does not have God; he who abides in the doctrine has both the Father and the Son.

The author now turns to apocalyptic language to describe the danger posed by the false teachers. His images are familiar from the warnings in 1 Jn 2:18-27 and 4:1-6—the former seems to predominate in the author's allusions. With the exception of the change in tense, v.7 reads like 4:2. The expression "deceivers" recalls 1 Jn 2:26 and "antichrist" applied to a person who will not confess that "Jesus Christ comes in the flesh," 2:18 and 4:3. We suggested (above on 1 Jn 4:2) that the author has modified a traditional christological formula "Jesus came/comes from the Father" to "in the flesh" as counter to his opponents' rejection of Jesus' death as atonement. But even in this context it remains unclear whether the modified formula would serve as a sufficient confessional test to identify false teachers. "Look to yourselves" (v.8) is common in apocalyptic preaching as a warning against falling victim to the snares that Satan will set up for the elect at the end of the age (Mk 13:5,9 par). Concern about losing/keeping one's reward also comes from apocalyptic preaching as the judgment saying in Mk 9:41 indicates. Paul shows such concerns for his own reward as an apostle when he admonishes his congregation to be faithful to the gospel as he has taught it to them (e.g. Gal 4:11). Within the context of Johannine eschatology, that reward, which could be lost, must refer to eternal life as in 1 Jn 2:25.

Verse 9 has more allusions to 1 Jn 2:22-27. Admonishments to "abide in" usually refer to the Father, Son or spirit; here, abiding in the doctrine of Christ (which probably means "about" Christ) makes it possible for a person to "have" the Father. Reference to the spirit's teaching the community occurs in a similar context in 1 Jn 2:27. 1 Jn 2:24 and 5:12 parallel the positive formulation in this passage. Perhaps, "goes ahead" refers to the people described as "having gone out from us" in 1 Jn 2:18. In any case, the point remains the same one the author has been making all along: no one who is not in unity with the tradition which the Johannine community has had from the beginning can claim to have salvation or to know the Father. This verse might apply not only to people actively spreading the false teaching but also to those who are inclined to listen to them.

NO FELLOWSHIP WITH FALSE TEACHERS.
10-11.

> [10]If any one comes to you and does not bring this doctrine, do not receive him into the house or give him any greeting; [11]for he who greets him shares his wicked work.

The author has finally come to the business of the letter: refuse all hospitality to those who teach a different doctrine; do not even speak with them. We will see in 3 Jn that a recommendation for the bearer can come in this position. The business of this letter makes it a parody almost! 1 Jn 5:14-21 invoked sanctions against the opponents indirectly, and we saw in discussing that passage that exclusion from the community in both essene and early christian rules often included the explicit statement that members were not to associate with such people. Such rules are presumably the basis of the author's request.

CONCLUSION.
12-13.

> [12]Though I have much to write to you, I would rather not use paper and ink, but I hope to come to see you and talk with you face to face, so that our joy may be complete. [13]The children of your elect sister greet you.

This conclusion is almost identical with 3 Jn 13f, which is one reason that those who are worried by the lack of specific address in this letter think that it may have been based on the content of 1 Jn and the format of 3 Jn. Verse 12 concludes with "that our joy may be complete"—very likely a reference to the opening of 1 Jn 1:4. It is typical of cultures which still rely on oral traditions to a large extent to consider written communication inferior to "face-to-face" encounter. People will apologize for writing or entrust the most important part of a message to the associate who brings the letter. Given the verbal identity between this conclusion and that of 3 Jn—with the exception of 12c—one cannot be sure if the author was actually contemplating a visit to the community in question. He may have been using a literary convention to back up his written exhortation with the suggestion of personal presence.

2 Jn does not offer us any substantively new information about the movement which led to the restatement of the tradition in 1 Jn. It does indicate, however, that Johannine christianity was spread about in several communities which were in frequent communication with each other. Both the author and his opponents might expect a hearing within the churches of the area in question. And, the author considers the threat of their teaching serious enough to seek to have other communities exclude such preachers from all forms of fellowship.

THREE JOHN

HOSPITALITY FOR
MISSIONARIES

Outline

SINCE 3 JN DEALS with a personal dispute between the
author and Diotrephes, apparently the leader of another
christian community, we find none of the elaborate appeal
to tradition—not even the love command—and few of the
allusions to other Johannine writings so typical of the
works against false teaching. The words which are unique to
this letter perhaps represent the author's private vocabulary
as opposed to the public language in which the tradition is
formally presented, though we will see enough of that public
language to feel confident that the author is the same person
who wrote 1 Jn. The body of the letter is more complex than
in 2 Jn, since the author wishes both to secure hospitality
for his associates (and perhaps himself) and to explain
Diotrephes' refusal to extend such hospitality.

(1) *Opening*: v.1.
(2) *Health wish*: v.2. Verses 3-4 add the thanksgiving
for the faith of the addressee which was characteristic of
the christian letter tradition.
(3) *Body*: vv.5-12.
    a) background, the addressee's reputation for hospi-
       tality vv.5-8
    b) Diotrephes' lack of hospitality, vv.9-10
    c) recommendation for Demetrius (request for
       hospitality) vv.11-12
(4) *Closing*: vv.13-15.

Although the opening of 3 Jn is the most secular of all the New Testament letters: the health wish is entirely conventional and there is no benediction. Other features resemble Pauline letter style: the recommendation is expanded with paraenesis (v.11); there is a longish thanksgiving (vv.3f); the author intends to deal with the failure of his earlier letter with a personal visit (v.10). These elements are so common in the Pauline corpus that some scholars have thought 3 Jn might have known Pauline letters. However, as we shall see, the problems mentioned in 3 Jn are so typical of those besetting travelling missionaries as they are illustrated in Paul's remarks about his own problems that one would expect closer analogies to Pauline style and language if actual Pauline letters lay behind the form of 3 Jn. 3 Jn probably represents the more common form of "letter of recommendation" carried by travelling missionaries to help them find hospitality in communities where they were not known. Paul tells the Corinthians that he does not need a letter of recommendation such as his opponents have (2 Cor 3:1f), since his congregation is his letter. The conventions of the secular letter were fairly stable over centuries. It is likely, therefore, that 3 Jn represents the conventional form of the missionary letter of recommendation. This form may have developed in christian circles before the great Pauline epistles (recognized even in their time to be something of a departure, so 2 Cor 10:10?) transformed the genre into a model of apostolic presence and preaching.

GREETING.
1.

> The elder to the Beloved Gaius, whom I love in the truth.

The usual "greeting" or a christian variant like "grace and peace to you" is missing from the opening. "Peace to you" occurs at the end of the letter instead (v.15). The description of the addressee as one "whom I love in truth" is identical with 2 Jn 1a and was probably the author's stock opening. "In truth" may only mean "truly" but it will form an *inclusio* with "walk in truth" at the end of the thanksgiving (v.4), which is typical of the author's style. Gaius was such a common name in antiquity that one cannot identify him with any of the others mentioned in the New Testament. Some people have thought that he must have been a member of the community headed by Diotrephes and liable to follow the latter's lead—hence the letter. However, the presentation of the background suggests that Gaius is unaware of the particulars of Diotrephes' action. Therefore, we assume that Gaius was the leader of another house-church in the same region as that of Diotrephes. It is clear that people from both groups travelled to and from the community in which the elder resides.

HEALTH WISH AND THANKSGIVING. 2-4.

> [2]Beloved, I pray that all may go well with you and that you may be in health; I know that it is well with your soul. [3]For I greatly rejoiced when some of the brethren arrived and testified to the truth of your life, as indeed you do follow the truth. [4]No greater joy can I have than this, to hear that my children follow the truth.

The health wish in v.2 is purely conventional. The RSV has over-translated the verse which concludes: "and that you may be healthy as you (lit. your soul) are well." "Soul" often, as here, does not refer to an entity separate from the body as the RSV handling of the sentence might suggest, but simply to the person addressed. All the author is saying is that he knows things are going well for Gaius (from the people who have reported about him) and he hopes that they continue to do so and that Gaius remains in good health.

Thanksgiving for the faith or christian conduct of the addressee is typical. The author uses the language of "walking in" (RSV "follow") truth found in 1 Jn 1:6f. This passage is similar to 2 Jn 4, but note that unlike both 1 and 2 Jn, there is no reference to the love command as such. Both 1 and 2 Jn stress it as part of their polemic against opponents whose teaching the author wishes to show is false to the tradition. Lack of such a reference here is another indication that the situation of 3 Jn is not that of 1-2 Jn.

The author has learned about Gaius' way of life from travelling missionaries. Perhaps they had also brought him the news about Diotrephes. The "my children" in v.4 has suggested to some that the elder had been a missionary and was responsible for Gaius' conversion or even for the establishment of the church in his area, since Paul uses "children" to refer to his converts (Phil 2:22; 1 Cor 4:14; Gal 4:19). However, though he does travel in the region, the elder never claims responsibility for the conversion of people there. "Children" was a common self-designation among Johannine christians (1 Jn 2:1,12,28; 3:7,18; 4:4; 5:12; 2 Jn 1,4), and the author is probably just using his normal way of speaking to those whom he exhorts. "My children" could refer to any christians in a community which would accept his teaching. We favor this interpretation of the verse, because it also seems that the reference to joy in it harks back to 1 Jn 1:4 where he has written testimony to the common tradition "that our joy may be full."

HOSPITALITY TO MISSIONARIES.
5-8.

> [5]Beloved, it is a loyal thing you do when you render any service to the brethren, especially to strangers, [6]who have testified to your love before the church. You will do well to send them on their journey as befits God's service. [7]For they have set out for his sake and have accepted nothing from the heathen. [8]So we ought to support such men, that we may be fellow workers in the truth.

Praising the hospitality of Gaius as well-known among travelling missionaries, sets the background to the body of the letter. Again notice that although hospitality is spoken of as love in v.6, the author does not invoke the love command as such. It was typical of the early christian mission that the beneficence of a congregation might be praised throughout an entire region. Paul speaks in a similar fashion of his own communities. Hospitality, as this passage points out, meant more than putting such people up. It also involved equipping them with whatever was necessary to continue their work. We have vivid examples of both the importance and the problems of obtaining such aid in the Pauline letters. Rom 15:22-26 tells a congregation to which he has no previous ties that Paul hopes to visit there and that he expects support for his missionary work further west. In 1 Cor 9:1-18, Paul defends both the practice of paying missionaries and his own refusal to take payment. But we learn from 2 Cor 11:8f that churches in Macedonia were contributing to his support while he was in Corinth preaching. Phil 4:14-17 are words of thanks to those christians for generous support not only when Paul was working among them, but also during his imprisonment. Phil 2:25 gives them the same title that 3 Jn 8 gives Gaius, "fellow worker." It seems clear that christians in settled communities were instructed to see themselves as sharing the work of evangelization (and in the Philippian case also the glories of apostolic suffering) by supporting the mission. Both the synoptic and Pauline traditions understand that obligation as derived from the teaching of Jesus himself (Mt 10:10 par; 1 Cor 9:14; 1 Tim 5:18). 3 Jn 7 insists that the christian mission be entirely self-supporting. The missionaries do not seek patronage or hospitality from pagan countrymen, though the stories in Acts suggest that at least the early missionaries must have done so—perhaps later converting their hosts. It would be usual for a person in a new area to seek out kinsmen, family friends, countrymen, or people of the same trade for assistance. If the christian missionaries are now to avoid receiving such assistance from "the heathen," then such "strangers" (v.3) must be able to count on local christian communities for help. The examples in Rom, 2 Cor and Phil are instructive. In Rom, Paul writes in advance to a community in which he is unknown to secure hospitality for himself and assistance with his future plans—or so he hopes. 2 Cor and Phil show that even communities indebted to the apostle's preaching for their faith might treat him in different ways. Some (Corinth) gave him no assistance even when he was present; others (Philippi and others in Macedonia) continued to support Paul's work when he was away from them by sending aid.

Thus, it becomes clear that although hospitality was held up as an ideal the actual realities of life made assistance of that sort, especially in a region where one was looked upon as a "stranger," of crucial importance. The generalization in v.8 "become fellow workers in the truth" may have been a standard part of the appeal for such assistance. Here "truth" does not refer to a specific doctrine or ethical precept but to the whole revelation of God in Jesus (in Pauline terms "the gospel"), which was being spread by the missionaries, "those who have gone out in his name" (RSV "for his sake"). "The name," i.e. Jesus', was a common way of referring to christianity in early missionary parlance (cf. Ac 4:17; 5:41; 1 Pet 4:6,16; Jn 15:21).

DIOTREPHES' INHOSPITALITY.
9-10.

> [9]I have written something to the church; but Diotrephes, who likes to put himself first, does not acknowledge my authority. [10]So if I come, I will bring up what he is doing, prating against me with evil words. And not content with that, he refuses himself to welcome the brethren, and also stops those who want to welcome them and puts them out of the church.

The Pauline examples provide good analogies for what is behind Diotrephes' action. The author must have written to a community centered around Diotrephes (perhaps meeting in his house) and requested support for some of his associates just as Paul is doing in Rom. That letter cannot have been 1 or 2 Jn, since it would have dealt with hospitality; not false teachers. It was probably a short letter of recommendation such as we have here in 3 Jn. Diotrephes both refused to give assistance on his own, and insisted that no one in his group do so either. Some commentators take "and puts them out of the church" to imply a formal excommunication against those who welcomed the missionaries. Perhaps, he simply was refusing to allow such people to come to meetings at his house.

None of the elaborate conflicts over church order that have been built on this passage seem well supported. Some have supposed Diotrephes to have been a monarchic bishop, who had excommunicated people, perhaps even Gaius and the elder. He has been held up as an example of a hardening orthodoxy, which found even the teaching of the elder too gnosticizing to fit the emerging consensus of faith the bishop was to defend. Or, alternatively, he has been cast as the successful gnostic opponent, who can do to the elder and his associates what the latter had tried to have done to him in 2 Jn. None of these constructions fits the fact that formal separation between the two groups does not seem to be involved. Nor does the author use his anti-opponent rhetoric. He still expects to pay Diotrephes a personal visit.

We noted in the introduction that it was typical of the time for people to be ambitious for power and honor and to use trade and religious associations to further those ambitions. Diotrephes may well have wished to establish his community as independent from those associated with the elder. Again, a passage from Paul may shed light on the situation. Phil 1:15-18 speaks of some people who have taken up preaching Christ out of rivalry. The fact that the apostle is in jail is in some way responsible for their doing so. Notice that unlike the opponents of Phil 3, Paul is not rejecting anything these people are preaching; he will even accept such preaching out of rivalry as long as Christ is preached (v.18). It seems clear, then, that some people have started preaching independently of the Pauline mission in the same area in which the apostle and his associates are working. The facts of the case in 3 Jn may be similar. Diotrephes may have decided to make his community an independent center of activity and to break off association with missionary activities centered in other churches. The RSV translation is a little misleading. Diotrephes does not "reject the authority" of the elder; he refuses to "receive (= welcome) us" (v.9), that is, he has denied hospitality to the elder or to his emissaries.

The elder accuses Diotrephes of "loving to be first." That unattested Greek verb may have been the author's own neologism fashioned on the basis of the adjective "love first place." Such expressions are typical of the rhetoric by which society controlled the ostentation of competitive and ambitious men. (Compare the condemnation of those who "love the first seats" in Mt 23:6 par). The expression has no relationship to any office Diotrephes might or might not have. 3 Jn goes on to claim that Diotrephes is doing evil by bringing false charges against the elder. (The RSV has translated a verb which has a technical meaning of "bring a false charge against" as "prating against"). We may presume that in denying the elder's request, Diotrephes had something to say against him. That would be even more the case if missionary associates of the elder were accustomed to pass through the area and stay with people there. He may even have used some of the "who does he think he is" rhetoric which underlies the "loving to be first" jibe by the elder. But anyone who recalls the bitter charges and countercharges between Paul and his opponents, the "super-apostles" of 2 Cor 10-13, or even the language used by the author against his opponents in 1 Jn, must find this a mild exchange indeed. The author does not even pull out his favorite "hating the brethren"—though you will notice that commentators almost unconsciously do so for him when interpreting 3 Jn, and thus miss the comparatively mild tenor of the letter.

RECOMMENDATION FOR DEMETRIUS.
11-12.

> [11]Beloved, do not imitate evil but imitate good. He who does good is of God; he who does evil has not seen God. [12]Demetrius has testimony from every one, and from the truth itself; I testify to him too, and you know my testimony is true.

Finally, the author comes to the immediate business of the letter, recommending Demetrius to Gaius. He first appeals to Gaius to continue the behavior for which he is known. And—lest there be any doubt as to the authorship of 3 Jn—he does so in language which has the overtones of the "official" speech of the Johannine community. Desirable behavior is "from God"; those who do otherwise "do not know God" (cp. 1 Jn 3:6,10; 4:4,6; 5:9). All the resonances of its expressions about testimony are used here simply to refer to the testimony provided by human recommendations (just as other missionaries had testified to the elder about Gaius, v.3). Presumably Demetrius is not one of the missionaries who had received hospitality from Gaius or a letter of recommendation would not have been required. He might have been previously excluded by Diotrephes and now requires a new base in the region.

CONCLUSION.
13-15.

> [13]I had much to write to you, but I would rather not write with pen and ink; [14]I hope to see you soon, and we will talk together face to face.
> [15]Peace be to you. The friends greet you. Greet the friends, every one of them.

Verses 13-14 are almost identical with 2 Jn 12, though the indication of a visit may not have been purely conventional. The author says that he expects to visit the area (v.10). He may also be using the occasion of 3 Jn to establish a welcome for himself with Gaius and his associates. The greetings to the "friends by name" (RSV "everyone of them") does not necessarily imply that the author has a large following in the area already. "Friend" was another self-designation in the Johannine community. (See Jn 15:14f where the departing Jesus who has commissioned his disciples to represent him in the world, now comes to call them friends.)

In its own way 3 Jn is a reflection of relationships between christians in this small network of communities of "friends." Personal ties of support and communication between churches are crucial to the spread of the mission, since there is no overarching structure of church authorities above the local groups or institution that might coordinate their interactions. It is no surprise to find as we do here that these groups were subject to the strains of interpersonal relations typical of a close-knit society of ambitious individuals. What is remarkable—even encouraging— about the example of these early christians is that a higher loyalty, a sense of responsibility for giving true testimony to the word of God, could be invoked in various ways to help people see the necessity of working through such divisions. At least, that could be the case so long as the divisions were not such that they destroyed the very fabric of true testimony and fellowship, itself—as is the case in 1-2 Jn. We do not know how the story of the elder and Diotrephes turned out. Pauline examples show that reconciliations were possible in instances with a much harsher rhetoric of opposition. It seems to us that the restraint of the author's remarks about Diotrephes, in contrast to what he has to say about the false teachers, is not a sign that the latter has greater ecclesiastical authority or is a successful gnosticizing leader, but is a sign that the author genuinely expects that a reconciliation will be effected. He is not out to alienate or cast off a fellow christian.

INSIGHTS FROM THE
JOHANNINE LETTERS

WHENEVER CHRISTIANS have had to confront challenges to their belief, they have developed new understand-
ings of the essential elements of their tradition. It is clear
that the Johannine author has not worked out a doctrine of
the relationship between divine and human in Christ as
it impinges on salvation. Some people have even found the
articulation of atonement theory in Hebrews superior to
1 Jn, since Heb tries to explain the necessity for Jesus'
humanity and obedience as an integral part of his having
offered the perfect sacrifice for sin. But the focus of the
discussion may have been such that the author did not feel
compelled to answer that question.

The spotlight on the relationship between Jesus and the
Father cast by the fourth gospel always inclines interpreters
to look for christology as the issue in Johannine writings.
The letters, in fact, back away from the spotlight and speak
much more often of God directly than does the gospel. Not
because they reject the insights of the gospel—they are too
imbued with its insights and language for that!—but because
Jesus in his relationship to God is not the issue. The letters
make clear that the Johannine church found more in its
tradition than Jesus, the revealer. It found a new sense of
God, and community. But what has shaken people is
apparently a new set of questions about their own salvation.
How were people pleasing to God? How did what had happened in Jesus effect their status with Him? How far did
forgiveness extend? Did the individual have to achieve a

heroic level of purity and ascetic holiness in order to gain eternal life? The author has focused on divine attributes, notably, "God is love" and tried to show how these attributes may be seen to be embodied in the community. Love, sinlessness, justice, perfection all belong to that community because God dwells with it.

We must constantly remember that ancient cities were small places. People all knew each other's business, and each other's conduct much more intimately than we do today. Perhaps in a small town or in the old quarters of Cairo or Jerusalem or in the villages of the Near East, one can gain some sense of what such a face-to-face society is like. The demands made on the christians by the expectation that their mutual love would reflect that of God manifested in Jesus could hardly be a matter of "private" conduct in such a context. Acts of both loving and hating the brethren would become matters of community knowledge even beyond christian circles. Thus, one should not think that a New Testament author's reference to "seeing your brother sin" meant that christians were going around prying into one another's lives. Everyday life in crowded streets—and most life takes place outdoors, in public—and crowded housing provides plenty of opportunity to observe one's brother.

The Johannine insistence that the community "show forth" what it means for God, who is invisible, to be love, perfect, righteous etc. is never presented as the achievement of community organization, as something which any group might achieve. 1 Jn sees the possibility of such relationships as dependent upon a christian "knowing God," that is, knowing that God has "first loved us" and has made perfection and forgiveness available through Jesus to those who belong to the christian community. In some respects, this community had to be uncharacteristic of other types of social association, since it demanded that its members transcend their normal social prejudices. Even their self-designation "friends" contrasts with the ancient view that one's friends were people like oneself in class, education, wealth etc. They claimed, on the other hand, that friendship was established by Jesus for all who believed in him. When we add to all this the strongly traditional character of graeco-roman society, which stressed family, status, hierarchy, competition, we begin to see that "loving one another" could have many ramifications. It was hardly a benign and pious reduction of the ethical teaching of Jesus to a single commandment.

We can also see the demands today that the church somehow be identifiable with the character of God as the one who seeks and saves the poor, the outcast, the captive, those denied human rights or whatever is another way of trying to realize a similar ideal. In our world there is a great contrast between small-scale individualism and private religious life and the large scale of institutions and bureaucracies, all magnified by electronic media. This contrast between our private small worlds and the large, visible media world "where the action is" makes it harder for christian communities to be meaningfully visible in the Johannine sense. I can think, for example, of many fine examples of just the kind of concern for neighbor that the Johannine writings insist show God's presence in the community, right here in my own parish. But many of these examples would not be known to the whole parish, let alone to the larger community in which we live. To try and broadcast them would not only be ludicrous, it would deprive them of the personal, human character which seems so fragile in our world. In the Johannine world, they would be known throughout the community. In our world, people have nothing else to focus on than the large-scale institutional gestures of a religious group and these turn out to be very difficult to endow with the sign value a Johannine understanding of church would seem to demand. 1 Jn would warn us that however we address the problem, we must also remember that human achievements and programs do not create the perfection and salvation about which he speaks; that has come as a gift from God.

1 Jn also faced a crisis of confidence. Christians were uncertain about whether salvation was theirs or not. Once again we have a crisis of confidence that the 20th century has magnified beyond anything the Johannine author might have imagined. Constant war and turmoil are certainly not foreign, but they have more powerful weapons of destruction; the possibility of "peaceful" nuclear accidents; global energy and economic crises painfully analyzed on T.V. everyday—all come together to convey the impression that the world is out of control. Secular and religious cults and saviors are all over the media. No one is very confident that our knowledge, our political and legal systems, our economy or any of our traditional values and religions can stem the rising chaos. So, people try the private sphere of self-help, meditation, devotion, anything that promises personal peace, freedom from stress, anxiety or whatever. And all too often this shift means giving up on the ills that beset the larger community. 1 Jn claims that real trust and confidence can only come from God's action toward the world as a whole. One cannot accept the attitude that there is only as much salvation or peace in the world as human beings manage to create for themselves. And, he also will not create confidence by indulging in the kind of doomsday preaching that assures a small group of the elect that this mess is about to end and all will be condemned except themselves. In the Johannine tradition, real confidence is grounded in the insight that Jesus' life and atoning death have broken the stranglehold of evil. And before we reject that idea with "that's easy for them to believe" we should remember how little of what we take for granted in tradition, social support, numbers, those Johannine christians had to nourish their faith.

Since that victory did not magically transform the world, it would have been meaningless without testimony. The Johannine community often seems so small and self-enclosed that we lose sight of its genuine missionary consciousness. We have seen the coming and going of missionaries among communities. Even the opponents who constitute such a danger are indication of a living dialogue of ideas. Testimony must also involve evaluation, since new expressions of faith cannot run counter to the fundamental insights of the tradition about the way in which Jesus shows God's love for humanity. We might also add that christians cannot have confidence in their salvation unless they have a sense that there is something important to say and bear witness to. And it will be in the nature of anything important or true that it will be opposed to things others may be saying. The Johannine example shows the absurdity of a common modern sentiment that every religious statement should be accepted if the person making it is sincere, really believes it. 1 Jn's opponents were sincere christians. 1 Jn does not even accuse them of being in it for the money—a common charge in ancient times as well as modern ones. The best he can do is to interpret their separation as "hating the brethren." Whatever their precise doctrine was, the implications of their preaching cannot be accepted. It seems to have destroyed people's confidence in their salvation, and perhaps, even undermined the vision of the love of God on which the Johannine community sees itself to have been founded. The author can still appeal to the community's own discernment of the tradition as they have learned it from the beginning to counter such preaching and lead them to true insight into what Jesus has accomplished. Christians today, perhaps, first need to understand some of these insights, what really has been handed on from the beginning, before they can figure out how to test the various modern spirits and how to witness the victory of Christ in today's world.

SUGGESTIONS FOR FURTHER READING

COMMENTARIES:

The following commentaries are written with the scholar in mind:

BROWN, R. *The Johannine Epistles.* (Anchor Bible #30). New York: Doubleday, forthcoming 1981.

BULTMANN, R. *The Johannine Epistles.* trans. R.P. O'Hara. Philadelphia: Fortress, 1973 (Ger[2] 1967).

SCHNACKENBURG, R. *Die johannesbriefe.*[4] (HTKNT XIII,3). Freiburg: Herder, 1970.

(For the moment the best modern commentary available.)

COMMENTARIES AIMED AT THE GENERAL READER:

DODD, C.H. *The Johannine Epistles.* New York: Harper, 1946. (Though without benefit of the newer Qumran and gnostic sources, still has useful suggestions for the general reader.)

HOULDEN, J.L. *A Commentary on the Johannine Epistles.* New York: Harper & Row, 1973.

SOURCE MATERIALS:

You can find the ancient writings referred to in the following:

Dead Sea Scrolls:

GASTER, T. *The Dead Sea Scriptures.*[3] New York: Doubleday / Anchor, 1976.

VERMES, G. *The Dead Sea Scrolls in English.*[2] Baltimore: Penguin, 1975.

Gnostic Writings:

ROBINSON, J.M. *The Nag Hammadi Library in English.* San Francisco: Harper/Leiden: E.J. Brill, 1977.
(= *NHLE* in the text, followed by the page).

Apostolic Fathers (Barnabas, Didache, Ignatius of Antioch):

LAKE, K. ed. & trans. *The Apostolic Fathers I.* Cambridge & London: Harvard/Loeb Classical Library, 1912 & many reprintings.

BOOKS AND ARTICLES:

BOGART,J. *Orthodox and Heretical Perfectionism in the Community.* Missoula: Scholar's Press, 1977.
(Useful survey of opinions about and background material for perfectionism in 1 Jn.)

BOISMARD, M.E. "The First Epistle of John and the Writings of Qumran." J.H. Charlesworth ed. *John and Qumran.* London: Goeffrey Chapman, 1972, 156-65.

BONNARD, P. "La première épitre de Jean est-elle johannique," *L'Evangile de Jean. Sources. rédaction, théologies.* (BETL 44). Gembloux: Duculot, 1977, 301-305.
(Useful discussion of the question of authorship.)

BROWN, R. *The Community of the Beloved Disciple.* New York: Paulist, 1979.
(An attempt to sketch out the whole history of the Johannine community; large section on the Johannine epistles.)

———, *The Gospel According to John I-XII; XIII XXI.* (AncBi #29; 29A). New York: Doubleday, 1966-70.
(Magisterial work on the fourth gospel. The reader of the letters will find appendices on key Johannine concepts useful.)

CAMPENHAUSEN, H. VON. *Ecclesiastical Authority and Spiritual Power in the Church of the First Three Centuries.* trans. J.A. Baker. Stanford: Stanford, 1969, pp. 12-123.
(Classic study of the development of church office; sees 3 Jn as representative of the conflict between emerging monarchic episcopate and older spiritual authority.)

CONZELMANN, H. "Was von Anfang war." *Neutestamentliche Studien fur Rudolf Bultmann.* (BZNW 21). Berlin: Topelmann, 1954, 194-201.
(On the connection between charism and interpretation of tradition in 1 Jn).

DONFRIED, K. "Ecclesiastical Authority in 2-3 John." *L'Evangile de Jean.* 325-33.

FORESTELL, T. *The Word of the Cross: Salvation as Revelation in the Fourth Gospel.* (AnaBib 57). Rome: Pontifical Biblical Institute Press, 1974.
(Helpful study of non-sacrificial interpretation of the death of Jesus in the Fourth Gospel.)

MALHERBE, A. "The Inhospitality of Diotrephes," *God's Christ and his People.* Fest. N. Dahl. ed. J. Jervell & W. Meeks. Oslo: Univesitet, 1977, 222-32.
————, *Social Aspects of Early Christianity.* Baton Rouge: Louisiana State, 1977, 60-70.
(On travelling and hospitality in early christianity.)

MARTYN, J.L. *History and Theology in the Fourth Gospel.*[2] Nashville: Abingdon, 1979.
(Important study of the relationship between the picture of Jesus in the gospel and the conflict with judaism.)

PERKINS, P. *The Gospel according to John: A Theological Commentary.* Chicago: Franciscan Herald Press, 1978.
(See the author's commentary for further explanation of the interpretation of the gospel behind its use here.)

VORSTER, W.S. "Heterodoxy in 1 John." *Neotestamentica* 9 (1975), 87-97.
(One of several recent articles warning against jumping into a gnostic interpretation of 1 Jn too quickly.)

ORAL CULTURES AND THEIR TRADITION:

The reader who would like more information about oral cultures and the transformation brought by literacy can begin with:

HAVELOCK, E.A. *Origins of Western Literacy*. Toronto: Ontario Institute for Studies in Education, 1976.

ONG, W. *Interfaces of the Word*. Ithaca: Cornell, 1977, 121-46 (on different modes of cognition); 230-71 (on biblical interpretation).

_____, *The Presence of the Word*. New Haven; Yale, 1967. (Fascinating study of media change and its impact on consciousness.)